Feminizing Hormonal Therapy
For The Transgendered

Second Edition - Copyright 1999 Together Lifeworks©

ISBN 1-887796-01-0

TABLE OF CONTENTS

TABLE OF CONTENTS (continued)

ABOUT THE AUTHOR

As a board certified gynecologic surgeon with over 25 years of medical experience in both private practice and research and as a T person herself, Dr. Sheila Kirk is in a unique position to help the Transgender Community improve their overall physical and emotional well-being while providing insight and instruction to the medical professionals who administer their care.

In 1998, Dr. Kirk made Trans-history by forming the only transgender surgical and medical center developed and directed by a Trans-surgeon. This center, known as TSMC, is the first of its kind in the world and is located in Pittsburgh, Pennsylvania. With the formulation of this unique center, Dr. Kirk became the first (and currently the only) Trans-surgeon performing MTF/FTM GRS and related surgeries for her community.

As a highly respected surgeon, Dr. Kirk has performed thousands of surgeries ranging from Genital Reassignment Surgery (GRS) and other related surgeries, hysterectomies, top surgeries, orchiectomies, breast augmentations to vaginal repair of all kinds and reconstructive gynecological operations. She is a leading expert in hormonal therapy for the MTF/FTM Trans population as well as for the peri-menopausal and post-menopausal natal woman.

One of Dr. Kirk's primary interests is in generating and promoting research in a number of areas regarding the care of the Transperson. Currently, Dr. Kirk is conducting two on-going research projects dealing with the teenage transgendered person and the post-operative MTF transsexual. In addition, she is currently in the process of developing research in contragender hormonal therapy as it relates to lipid profiles and potential cardiac disease in the FTM individual and breast and prostate problems in the MTF individual.

A noted author and lecturer, Dr. Kirk has written numerous books, articles and research findings on transgendered care as well as other medical concerns in her chosen discipline.

Sought after worldwide as a leading authority on transgender issues, Dr. Kirk, lectures extensively at universities, medical conferences and symposiums. In 1997, Dr. Kirk became the first Trans surgeon to be elected to the board of the Harry Benjamin International Gender Dysphoria Association. In that capacity, she has co-established a committee of Advocacy and Liaison to encourage better communication and understanding of the healthcare needs of her community and to better convey that information to the professionals who administer their care.

You can reach Dr. Kirk the following ways:

E-mail: SheilaKirk@aol.com
Phone: (412) 781-1092

Snail Mail:
Sheila Kirk, M.D.
P.O. Box 38366
Pitttsburgh, PA 15238-9998

Or visit our website at:
www.tsmccenter.com

Other Publications by Sheila Kirk, M.D.:

MASCULINIZING HORMONAL THERAPY FOR THE TRANSGENDERED
©1996 Together Lifeworks, Pittsburgh, PA
ISBN 1-887796-02-9

MEDICAL, LEGAL AND WORKPLACE ISSUES FOR THE TRANSSEXUAL
Sheila Kirk, M.D and Martine Rothblatt, J.D.
©1995 Together Lifeworks", Pittsburgh, PA
ISBN 1-887796-00-2

PHYSICAN'S GUIDE TO TRANSGENDERED MEDICINE
©1996 Sheila Kirk, MD, Pittsburgh, PA
ISBN 1-887796-03-7

HORMONES - MALE TO FEMALE
©1994 edition Sheila Kirk, M.D
(English/German/French/Spanish Translations)

HORMONES - FEMALE TO MALE
©1994 edition Sheila Kirk, M.D.
(English/German/French/Spanish Translations)

HORMONAL TREATMENT FOR THE TRANSSEXUAL-AN OVERVIEW FOR THE PROFESSIONAL (AUDIO CASSETTE)
©1994 Sheila Kirk, M.D.

HORMONES-MALE TO FEMALE, FEMALE TO MALE
©1991,1992 editions Sheila Kirk, M.D.

HOW TO FIND A PHYSICIAN
©1989 Sheila Kirk, M.D.

HOW TO BE A GOOD MEDICAL CONSUMER
©1989 Sheila Kirk, M.D.

I'm exceedingly grateful to Pamela, my Life Partner, for her knowledgeable review and contribution to the assembling of this 1999 edition and for her very expert involvement in the previous edition as well. Without her expertise and insight I could never accomplish a work such as this. Her great knowledge and very perceptive contributions have elevated all my writing and my lectures as I have produced them for my community for the past five years.

In earlier editions of the hormone Treatises, I had remarkable assistance from two others. I wish to thank Lori, my office assistant for many years. I am very grateful for her generous assistance in the preparation of much of the basic material that was preparatory to this edition. I want also to thank my very capable transcriptionist, Joan for her tireless effort and patience with me in assembling so much of my literary efforts.

Last, let me thank the many hundreds of brothers and sisters who have shared with me their experiences using a contra-hormonal regimen. And particularly those who have been my patients in that experience. I hope I have given to your knowledge as much as you have given to mine.

Sheila Kirk, M.D.

The Future Is Ours

The title of this Foreword was inspired by a statement sent to me by a person who was kind enough to express their support of the opening of my Trans surgical center. It is one of hundreds of positive remarks and encouragement I have received from community members, Trans and non-Trans healthcare professionals and others since forming the Transgender Surgical & Medical Care Center (TSMC). These encouraging remarks have been most gratifying and it reinforces my reasons for building the center. "Thank you, Dr. Kirk, your courageous step has helped to insure that the future of our medical & surgical care can at last, be ours." This statement so struck me because it succinctly expresses what my intentions were when I began pulling all the many complex pieces together to formulate TSMC. It was my intention then, as is now, as it will always be, to provide the highest standards of care, concern and management throughout all stages of your surgical and medical needs. But equally as important to all of us in our community, TSMC was founded with another purpose in mind. It is my firm belief that in order to achieve complete healthcare empowerment then we must not only be surgical/medical consumers but we must also be afforded the right to be our own surgical/medical providers. This is not to say that we should not recognize or support many of those non-T professionals who have worked so hard to educate themselves in healthcare circumstances unique to us and who provide us with sound, compassionate care and management. But what it does mean, is that we should have an opportunity to select Trans professionals to manage and care for our entire healthcare needs through all stages of our gender journey.

Unfortunately, we all know that at present that is not the case. Although some important headway has been made by our sisters and brothers in the psychologic fields, many of us are aware of the difficulties encountered by medical physicians who have been forced or asked to leave their hospitals, their residencies or their medical partnerships when they come out or when they transition. Some have been able to continue caring for us in solo office settings, some have opened clinics that offer out-patient cosmetic surgical services but very few have been able to maintain their hospital privileges and work within the system in the discipline in which they were trained. And until the start of TSMC no Trans surgeon has performed GRS and related surgical procedures for members of our community.

Yes, it is rewarding to me to be the first surgeon who was able to break the barrier that permeates the medical profession but that accomplishment has bittersweetness about it. Trans-medical professionals treating our community at all levels should be the **norm** not the **exception**.

How can this be accomplished? It won't be an easy task. But if we want empowerment and the ability to make important decisions in our healthcare needs, it needs to be done. We must all unite together, support each other and work together to help those who wish to work within the healthcare system. And support them when they do. Statistics show that when given the choice genetic women (GW) prefer to have GW physicians and psychologists treat them. We can go a long way to empowering ourselves just as GW's have empowered themselves by enlisting Trans-professionals to administer our care. I am not suggesting, however, that we should go to T professionals simply because they are members of our community. That would be foolhardy and potentially hazardous to our health. *Select your Trans professional with the same concern and guidelines you would any other healthcare provider.*

Another way we can help one another is by mentoring one another. Those of us who are physicians and mental healthcare providers can help those who are considering working in the medical field or who wish to enter it by sharing their expertise and life experience. Many of my colleagues, as well as myself, do this already in an informal manner but a more united effort could prove to be much more helpful and effective.

xx

TSMC is committed to going a step further. We are dedicated to improving upon the informal mentoring that surgeons performing GRS surgeries worldwide now provide one another. Many of you may be surprised to learn that GRS surgeons learn from one another through observation and assisting in each other's surgeries, by sharing their techniques with each other and by reporting to the medical literature and at meetings. Currently there is no formal training program in Trans-surgery; informal mentoring and exchange with other surgeons is the method that is used by all who work in this surgical discipline. We, at TSMC, feel that our community would be better served by instituting a formalized program. Therefore, as we grow, we will formally teach the intricate techniques of trans-surgeries, our pioneered techniques and our methods to improve sensation and functionality to talented and dedicated residents wanting to make this important discipline their career choice in the future. We intend to do our part in empowering our community not only by providing the best and most innovative care and surgical technique but also by training Trans (and non-T) individuals interested in making Trans surgery and medicine their professional future.

This step is a first step for our community...a small step ... when compared to the others steps that should and will follow in this relatively new discipline I like to refer to as **Trans Care**. So much needs to be done and it will take the commitment and support of all of us. Yet, it is a much-needed step towards our empowerment and one that is far overdue. Where are we to go from here? It's up to us to decide.

Empowerment on the medical and surgical level isn't the only task at hand toward our independence and self-reliance. Take a moment to think about how you might be able to help our community help ourselves. Each of us has a special gift, a unique ability, a much-needed skill that can go a long way in helping us strengthen ourselves and to insure that there truly is a "unity within our community."

Yes...the future is ours. And it can be a bright, promising one if we all work together to make it happen.

A Renegade Working Within The System

In some ways, I am totally traditional and follow concepts and precepts that I learned in my early training as a medical student, clinging to them firmly. Some of them I have abandoned altogether. A few have been altered to fit a new era of medical and surgical care. I have tried to modify my approach to actual and potential patients, and to fit their individual needs with the new methods and advances in medical knowledge that are currently available.

Medicine is truly an art. Yet it has blended with it, such a remarkable body of science so as to make it still gratifying, rewarding and even thrilling to both the recipient and the provider. Both profit and reap the reward in most instances. Still there is caution to both of these, the recipient and the provider, that realism and sensible expectation must be mixed with the treatment. Both have the responsibility to work together and to understand as much as possible, the means as well as the end.

I remember still what I was told by one of my medical lectures in my surgical clinic rotation at Boston City Hospital years ago. "Be not the first by whom the new is tried; yet not the last to lay the old aside." The middle road is the first suggestion that comes to mind in this guideline, but really that is not altogether true. It means alertness to change. Awareness to innovation but with caution to implement until there is evidence to embrace the new. It means to be ready to alter techniques and rules that could positively change as the patient and societal needs change.

Employing that approach, I could be called a "renegade" in some circumstances. I very often treat individuals with low dose medication or consider strongly orchiectomy (removal of the testes) for others even when my colleagues would recoil at my decisions (Chapters 11 & 14). At the same time, I hold tightly still to the principle that all who take the step to feminizing therapy need proper evaluation and monitoring to insure health and well-being. This makes some in our Community recoil as well, for philosophy that some hold dearly is that they should self-treat and don't need medical monitoring. Their bodies are their own.

With this mix of liberalism and traditional, I write for you, my dear reader, what I know is a sensible, effective and knowledgeable approach to feminizing treatment. I want you to **13** benefit and to find success in your journey toward your goals, and at the same time, I want you to be informed and able to make intelligent decisions on your own personal journey. Take my liberal and traditional mixture as it is intended, to give you information. Your decisions are yours but should not be based on folly and whim but rather on sound medical principles and education.

Sheila Kirk, MD
Pittsburgh, Pennsylvania
July, 1999

Through the years, a moderate amount of reporting of hormonal therapy for the transgendered person has found its way into the various medical journals. In years past, the data was helpful to health-care professionals who care for the transgendered, but it was based on experience with small groups of individuals receiving therapy of various kinds. In recent years, medical reporting, while coming from a precious few researchers throughout the world, is much more meaningful based on larger series of transgendered individuals observed for longer periods of time. This is what is important in developing therapy techniques of all kinds, and it is very much the case with hormonal therapy of the transgendered male to female person.

This book is for you, the transgendered person, truly not for your doctor. Your physician has access to the medical literature. Though I do understand how some medically trained can find this information of help in their care of you, the medical literature is available to them for more in-depth concept and information.

The information compiled here for **your** review and education is presented in simple language purposefully for your complete understanding and for your ability to be able to discuss all aspects of care with your physician. This information is based on medical research and reporting to the medical community. It is not taken from the transgendered literature which often carries with it myth, misinformation, and fantasy. With this in mind, what I am telling you is what is told to physicians when they read medical studies to educate themselves, to give better care to you. They are accustomed to scientific language and detail. I will try very hard not to burden you with that kind of detail.

The data I give to you is meant to inform, not to frighten. I believe that most candidates for hormonal therapy can use a hormonal regimen with a high degree of safety, as long as they are evaluated adequately for hormonal use and then monitored on a regular basis so as to be certain that good health is maintained. This concept is supported in the medical literature.

It is very important, as well, that patients on hormonal regimens adhere to the instructions given to them by their physicians.

There are some precepts that must be emphasized at the very start, however, and they are meant to safeguard you, and to instill in you, a deep sense of reality as you follow this pathway to a contragender existence:

1. I want to give a very strict warning to those who would consider using hormonal medication prescribed for another person. This is **not** safe! Do not do it! **Ever!**

2. A similar and even more forceful caution is given to those who would purchase their hormones from a black market source. Also purchase of these medications from mail order houses that sell to anyone making inquiry could be a problem. To purchase from sources in foreign countries and from vendors who claim that they can "get it for you", is a calculated risk. They are, in essence, pill pushers and very suspect in whatever they offer. The medication may not be pure. It may be contaminated. In essence, it could cause you great harm. Even more importantly, medication whether oral or injectable obtained this way, will tempt one to bypass the important monitoring rendered by a qualified and knowledgeable medical physician. This can only lead to very serious consequences. **Don't do it!** Some approaches to mail order can be less expensive without doubt, but be certain of your choice and **don't self-medicate.** You need your physician to monitor you.

3. I urge you to take your prescriptions to a reputable pharmacy and to abide by the instructions given to you for their use. Don't double dose or alter the regimen without discus-

sion with your doctor for this, can lead to serious problems. There should be room for discussion with your physician, and the doctor with experience in transgendered medical care, in particular, should know there are many ways to accomplish what is possible for you.

Individuals who do not follow these guidelines are risking their health. Granted, physicians who care and who are responsible and empathetic are not always easy to find—but they do exist. If you are tempted to take shortcuts or abbreviated pathways, please remember that good health is paramount and you must preserve it. Anything that risks good health is foolhardy and irrational.

The plan for this book is to give some insight into the subject of endocrinology, a branch of internal medicine that deals with special glands in our bodies, which produce hormones. Quite specifically, we will deal with the sex hormones, estrogen and progesterone. Testosterone antagonists, known as anti-androgens, will be discussed as well since they are part of some feminization regimens. To provide a little more background, we will describe briefly some of the anatomy and some of the biochemistry involved with production of the sex hormones, also known as sex steroids.

Next, we will discuss some of the physiology or function of the sex hormones, estrogen and progesterone, in the genetic female and discuss what they do for her. We will discuss how these hormones counteract testosterone in the genetic male and alter the physical changes brought about by testosterone production through in their pubertal years. This, in fact, is the feminization process.

Following this, we will discuss complications or problems encountered in hormonal use in the genetic male and give insight into some of the hormonal regimens currently in use throughout the world.

The medical evaluations, both the initial exam and periodic monitoring, will be discussed and the methods for taking measurements will be demonstrated. Self-breast examination is a technique you should learn and conduct regularly. A guide for this will be provided.

Important and frequently asked questions have been included and answered. These questions quite possibly could be ones you have wanted to have answered but didn't know where to get accurate and honest answers.

New information has been included in various chapters out-lining important new research findings. Dr. Becky Allison's recent medical paper has been included because of its great importance in evaluation and maintenance of candidates for hormonal treatment. We are most grateful to her for her work in this important area.

Several new chapters have been added. Discussions of or-chiectomy (removal of the testes), low dose therapy and natu-ral occurring therapy are especially important with trends and new indications for these modes of treatment becoming very evident.

Again, my intent is to give you basic, accurate knowledge so you can work more cooperatively with your physician and better understand his or her approach to you and allow you to become an active participant in many decisions.

A Little Anatomy and Biochemistry

To begin with, we ought to define the word **hormone**, since they are such common and special substances in the human body. Their involvement in human physiology is quite extensive, for they are a part of the growth and daily maintenance of the human body. Hormones are what reproduction is all about. But even more, hormones are necessary to our health and the quality of our lives because they are a part of so many other physiologic systems.

A hormone is a complex chemical structure made in very minute amounts in specialized organs called glands. It is deposited directly into the bloodstream and is transported in a special manner to a target organ. There it exerts a very special and specific influence upon that target organ. The target organ may be another hormone gland or a non-hormonal body tissue. The hormone enters that structure and influences it to function in a particular manner.

The target organ under such an influence will act to produce an activity or function. For instance, consider the female's uterus. It is a target organ that responds to the hormones estrogen and progesterone as they are produced in her hormone gland, the ovary. (The ovaries themselves are target organs for the pituitary gland.) Under the influence of estrogen and progesterone on a cyclic basis, the lining of the uterus responds in specific ways to prepare for a pregnancy. If pregnancy does not take place, the lining of the uterus will eventually change to a point where it will disintegrate and slough away. This is known as the menstrual period, and it is a fairly regular process for most females during their reproductive years.

Special glands in our bodies then make these hormones. They make up the **Endocrine System**, and they are under the auspices of a master endocrine gland called the pituitary located very close to the brain. The pituitary gland produces hormones that are called **gonadotropins**. They are specific to each endocrine gland. They enter the blood stream and are taken to the other endocrine glands by an elaborate transport system. The **gonadotropins** stimulate those glands to produce their own hormones, which in turn then exert effect upon other target organs such as skin, bone, muscle, breast, reproductive tract structures, and a host of other tissues. The hormones activate the target structures by a very special system located on the surfaces of the many thousands of cells forming the target organ. This system is composed of receptors which either accept or reject the hormone presented. If accepted, the hormone enters each cell and causes reaction(s) that are characteristic for that target organ or tissue. It's very complicated but very efficient and exceedingly important to good health, for as you will see in the following, hormones enter into many body systems, not just those that have to do with being male or female.

Let's list the endocrine glands of the human body:

The Pituitary Gland

Located on the undersurface of the brain, it makes a number of gonadotropic hormones. The **pituitary gland** is itself under the control of the **hypothalamus**, a part of the brain. In a complex relationship with the endocrine glands, it influences them to regulate the amounts of hormones they characteristically produce.

Gonadotropin Hormones Made By The Pituitary

Thyroid Stimulating Hormone

Parathyroid stimulating hormone

Adrenal stimulating hormones

Ovarian stimulation hormones -follicle stimulating hormone and luteinizing hormone

Testes stimulating hormones -follicle stimulating hormone and luteinizing hormone

Growth hormone - most prominent at puberty

The Thyroid Gland

This gland is located in the neck near to the "Adam's apple." The pituitary gland directs the thyroid to produce hormone that has influence upon metabolism. Along with growth and maintenance of body tissues, it has a great deal to do with reproduction in the genetic female. Lack of adequate thyroid function leads to many changes in the body in gastrointestinal adequacy and in the maintenance of the skin, for example. The condition known as **hypothyroidism** can affect many systems and processes that rely on thyroid hormone to function correctly for good health. Overactivity in this gland leads to very serious disease changing normal cardiac functions to abnormal ones.

The Parathyroid Glands

These glands, four in number, are located in the neck just in front of the thyroid gland. Their hormone production is involved with calcium and phosphorus metabolism, and therefore, they are vital to skeletal growth and overall bone metabolism throughout our entire lives.

The Adrenal Glands

These glands, two in number, are located in the back of the torso on the very top of each kidney. Hormones from these glands are very involved with glucose (carbohydrate) metabolism and water and electrolyte balance. Electrolyte balance is vital to a healthy cardiac function, to kidney and musculoskeletal activity and to various enzyme systems, to name only a few. Certain conditions of adrenal overactivity can lead to diabetes. Underactivity of certain adrenal functions can lead to death. They produce in small amounts the sex hormones, estrogen and testosterone as well.

The Ovarian Glands

There are two **ovaries** in the normal genetic female and they are located deep in the lower abdomen (pelvis,) next to the **uterus**. The major hormones they produce, **estrogen** and *progesterone*, are not only part of the reproductive tract, but are intimately involved in many other organ systems and bodily functions. Bone metabolism, regulation of blood cholesterol, the breasts and the skin are only a few of the other systems that depend upon the ovarian sex hormones in adequate supply.

The Testicular Glands

The *testes* are located in a sac outside of the body called the *scrotum*, just beneath the penis. The major hormone, *testosterone*, produced in the testes is not only part of reproductive tract function, but very involved in many other organ systems and body functions. Musculature, bone metabolism, cholesterol levels in the blood, red blood cell production and much more depend on it. Some cells in the testes produce testosterone and other androgenic hormones. Some cells, however, produce sperm cells which fertilize the female egg to begin a pregnancy.

The *Pituitary* has influence in several other systems which certainly can be considered as part of the endocrine system:

Prolactin - A hormone made in the pituitary that takes part in the development of the female breast in puberty and which is the main influential factor in the production of breast milk during and after pregnancy. However, it is produced in males as well as females, though in much, much lower amounts.

Pancreas - The pituitary gland is in balance with this organ in its production of insulin and with the adrenal gland in their hormonal influence upon glucose metabolism. If the balance is altered a diabetic state or a blood sugar deficit state (hypoglycemia) will develop.

Placenta - This organ though only a temporary one formed in a pregnancy, is a virtual factory of hormone production. It assumes influence over the maintenance of the pregnancy replacing ovarian hormone support after a certain early period of time in the pregnancy. This is in addition to its necessary activity in conducting nutrition and oxygen to the developing fetus.

At the risk of being too scientific, I'm going to show you the biochemical scheme for the production of **progesterone**, **testosterone**, and **estradiol** (estrogen) in the genetic female and the genetic male. Certain enzyme systems and pathways in the female are more active by genetic determinism such that estrogen and progesterone are produced in decidedly greater quantities than in the male. However the female also produces a small amount of testosterone. In the genetic male, the pathway for testosterone production is much more active, and his production of estrogen and progesterone is considerably less. Genetic influence determines prominence of one system over another, just as it does in the embryologic beginnings and then development of certain anatomic structures specific for males and females.

Note also that cholesterol is the precursor, or original chemical substance from which all the hormones come. Our bodies can make two carbon segments (acetyl groups) and chemically join them together to make cholesterol from which come many different substances needed in our bodies, including the hormones testosterone, estradiol (estrogen), and progesterone. Our bodies, however, prefer to use dietary cholesterol in various "breakdown" reactions to make the three hormones. Cholesterol is very important to us, for it takes part in some way in the metabolism or function of virtually all tissue in our bodies. The much-publicized concern over it, has to do with its excess in our systems and the "pile up" in our arteries leading to vessel and heart disease. As the saying goes— "Too much of a good thing ..."

Now this is a very complicated chemical scheme, yet this very complex set of reactions goes on daily in the ovaries and in the testes, and to a small extent as well in the adrenal glands of both sexes. The production of these three hormones depends upon pituitary control, as we have noted before, and when released into the blood for reaction with other tissues, these hormones are transported to various organs. They enter at the cellular level of those organs under very special circumstances and complex reactions. This is the receptor mechanism we spoke of. Once the hormones have been used in the

Formation of Sex Steroids From Cholesterol

Acetate

Cholesterol

20 hydroxylase
22 hydroxylase
20, 22 desmolase

17α-hydroxylase

Pregnenolone

3β-ol-dehydrogenase
Δ⁴⁻⁵ isomerase

17-Hydroxypregnenolone

Progesterone

desmolase

17α-hydroxylase

Dehydroepiandrosterone

17-Hydroxyprogesterone

3β-ol-dehydrogenase
Δ⁴⁻⁵ isomerase

desmolase

Androstenedione

17β-ol-dehydrogenase

Testosterone

aromatization

aromatization

Estrone

17β-ol-dehydrogenase

Estradiol

target organ appropriately, they are again returned to the blood and transported to more tissues that are in need of them. Hormones are unchanged when promoting or facilitating tissue reaction. They can be used again and again until destroyed by specific body processes. Estrogen is usually transported to the liver for breakdown. In contrast, testosterone is most often catabolized or broken down in the target organ cells. The breakdown products from both sites are excreted in urine, bile and fecal waste.

24 All three of these hormones are in the bloodstream of males and females at all times. As we have noted, progesterone, testosterone, and estrogen are present in different concentrations in males and females. The concentrations also vary from one time to another dependent upon physiologic need. All three are in free form in very small amounts, but the greatest amounts are bound to serum proteins and are released as the need is made known by the cells of the body. As mentioned, the transport to, and transport across some membranes, is intensely complex and are a tribute to the wonder, the mystery, and the phenomenal organization of our bodies. The biochemical reactions that take place are truly remarkable.

It should be emphasized that generally destruction or breakdown of these hormones in the various cells of the body, in specific the liver cells, is efficient and without harm to the individual in the short or in the long term. It is the damaged liver (from infection, alcohol and substance abuse) that has a real problem with hormonal breakdown and disposal. A healthy liver manages these processes quite well.

- *Hormones are produced in special organs known as the Endocrine Glands*

- *Hormones influence other organs and tissues to function*

- *The Female hormones (Estrogen and Progesterone) come from the ovaries and the adrenal glands of genetic females and testes and adrenals of genetic males but in very different amounts*

  25

- *Hormones are vital in maintaining good health and activity*

The Hormones —
Estrogen and Progesterone in the Genetic Female

The young female, up to the average age of 12 years, has about the same body shape (habitus), the same voice pitch, the same daily organ system function, as does her young male counterpart. Her pituitary gland has been active, providing stimulus to other endocrine glands to continue development, growth, and normal physiology, but there has been no real influence on her reproductive organs. Usually between the ages of 10 and 13, a pituitary hormone we call a gonadotropin that is specific to the ovaries will start stimulating the special cells in the ovary to begin their cyclic activity in producing the sex hormone estrogen (estradiol). That gonadotropin is called **follicle stimulating hormone**. Once this interaction begins, the pituitary and the ovary will maintain a relationship of changing influence upon each other in an ever recurrent cyclic manner for all of the reproductive years and for some variable time beyond when menopause is complete.

With the beginning of ovarian activity, only estrogen is produced. The responses it engenders are dramatic. This is the pubertal time for the female. During this phase, hair growth begins in the arm pits and the pubic area, fat stores are redistributed, and her body shape becomes very characteristically female. Her torso assumes more of the "hour glass" appearance. Long bone growth is actually halted, and stature is fixed under the influence of estrogen. The skin and scalp hair change and most notably, her breasts begin to develop having more size, volume and shape. In entering puberty she begins her journey into womanhood. After a year or so of these alterations, the pituitary gland exerts more of its influence upon the ovaries. Another gonadotropin, **luteinizing hormone**, is produced, stimulating special cells in the ovary to produce progesterone and to make eggs. This process, called ovulation, now causes her to be fertile and she can now reproduce. She then has an instinctual drive to conceive. She may have had some uterine bleeding to this point (anovulatory periods), but now as she begins ovulatory function on a regular basis, her menstrual period will now become more regular. She will continue to ovulate and menstruate alternately until her mid 40's or early 50's, at which time she will have a loss of ovarian activity (menopause) and a gradual and then almost complete loss of production of estrogen and progesterone.

All through the years of estrogen production many other organ systems have benefited and have been maintained under the influence of estrogen. To give only one important aspect of estrogenic activity consider the following: *Estrogen* is very much a part of the lipid, or fat metabolism in the female. It influences the levels of cholesterol in the blood, as well as the important transport substances for cholesterol, the lipoproteins known as LDL and HDL. These substances have a great deal to do with the development of *arteriosclerosis*, or atheromatous plaque formation in the arteries, particularly in the arteries of the heart. Estrogen retards the development of this vessel disease more commonly known as "hardening of the arteries." The genetic female develops cardiovascular disease at a much slower rate in her life while she is producing estrogen. This is in contrast to her male counterpart who develops arteriosclerosis at earlier ages.

All aspects of her femininity and continuing good health will be contributed to by her estrogen production. In every female's life there will be a time when she will begin to undergo changes in pituitary and ovarian activity and estrogen and progesterone production will be altered. As she grows older she moves into the menopausal phase of her life. She will make less and less estrogen and ovulate much more seldom with subsequent loss of fertility.

In addition, there is often a diminished libido, and eventually a loss altogether of her menstrual periods. As one looks at the aging female, there are very notable alterations in her skin and in her hair. There will be changes in the position and size of her breasts and distinct changes in subcutaneous fat storage and distribution. Her bone metabolism will change and she then becomes susceptible to a condition known as **osteoporosis**. The danger of bone fracture increases with time because of this change in the bones, brought about by the loss of estrogen support. Her stature and posture will reflect this as well. She may demonstrate the characteristic 'Widow's Hump' in her upper back. Her cholesterol metabolism will be altered considerably, and she now becomes a candidate for blood vessel change and the accelerated development of heart disease. In fact, women well into menopause and beyond, experience the same changes in coronary artery plaque disease that males experience at an earlier age. The mortality rates for women due to heart disease catch up to that of men who don't have this natural protection and began this process some time before. In later life, women die more because of heart disease than any other disorder, even cancer.

Now don't believe that it is only due to estrogen that the female remains sound and healthy. There are hundreds of other influences that give her the appearance and good health she enjoys. Good nutrition, exercise, freedom from infection and stress, sound living habits and genetic influences and many other things, account for good health. But the influence of estrogen in the reproductive years can't be stressed enough. Estrogen in the female serves her very well. It is vital to her reproductive apparatus, but even more, it gives her a longer and better quality of life while her body produces it. This is the rationale for why women should use estrogen in the perimenopausal and postmenopausal phases of their life, for it continues the good effects that they have experienced while producing estrogen in their own ovaries at younger ages.

What of **progesterone**? What does it do for her in her reproductive years? It does have great importance, for it is very necessary to reproduction and to maintenance of a progressive healthy pregnancy, as well as the maintenance of other organs (i.e., breasts). It should be noted however, that it does tend to have an "androgenic" or testosterone-like effect in some instances, and when taken in medicine, i.e., birth control pills, it could counteract the benefits of estrogen in the genetic female to some extent. Years ago some contraceptive medication contained certain synthesized (laboratory made) progesterones that had notable androgenicity, and they negatively influenced lipid metabolism. That influence altered cholesterol and triglyceride levels in the blood and changed LDL and HDL ratios. All of this raised the fear in physicians of increasing risks of arteriosclerotic vessel disease, along with changing certain clotting factors in the blood. In truth, there were in the medical literature reports of increased numbers of heart attack and strokes in women using these contraceptives. Progesterone is not all as positive as is estrogen, particularly so when it is incorporated in various medications. Yet its production in the ovaries is essential and very important to the genetic female in a number of ways.

Of late, studies have been reported that link estrogen with **Alzheimer's Disease**, a neurodegenerative disease of the brain that causes a slow, progressive loss of mental function. Currently, 4 million people, male and female, in the United States have this disorder. By 2030, the number affected will double. Hence, it constitutes a real public health problem for the future. Five recent medical studies have consistently demonstrated a 40% to 60% reduction in the relative risk of Alzheimer's disease in post-menopausal women who use estrogen. Its also a suspicion though not entirely proven that women with the disease may have improved cognition if estrogen is taken in later decades of life. When studying women who experience "hot flashes" in the menopausal years because of lack of estrogen, it is hypothesized that there is a loss of neurons (nerve cells) in the brain such that when they are 70 or 80 years old, these women are more likely to demonstrate Alzheimer's and even to exhibit early signs at younger ages. The use of estrogen in those earlier years to control hot flashes seems to lessen the incidence of Alzheimer's or modify and slow its progression.

✖✖✖

- *Estrogen is a hormone in the genetic female that is produced at puberty and continues to be functional until menopause*

- *Estrogen's influence extends into many physiologic systems from the formation of the female body shape, to the maintenance of her bones and the reduction of cardiovascular risk.*

- *Estrogen's involvement in many body functions is essential for her good health and fertility*

- *Progesterone is necessary in the genetic female for adequate menstrual function and fertility but its importance is not as overall crucial to her well-being as estrogen*

The Hormone Testosterone in the Genetic Male

Let's consider the young male who is prepubertal. His pituitary gland has been active and functioning in the many ways that it has in the prepubertal female, but he is growing and maturing at a somewhat slower pace. At a chosen time for him, puberty begins just as notably as it does for the female. The pituitary will produce the gonadotropins, **follicle stimulating hormone**, and **luteinizing hormone** which will stimulate the testes to develop and function. This will result in the production of testosterone, which along with growth hormone from the pituitary and thyroid hormones, will now produce a young man who becomes tall, husky, and athletic. His muscles increase in size and in strength. His chest expands, and his waist is in line with his hips. Hair growth is noticeable on his arms, chest, armpits, legs, face and around the genitalia. His voice deepens. His penis lengthens, and with increasing frequency, it becomes erect spontaneously. There is nocturnal discharge of milky material, an ejaculate which will soon contain thousands of sperm. He becomes aggressive and dominant. His thoughts turn to the female. He is oriented to sexual encounters. His instinct tells him that this is very important to his enjoyment of life. He is male, with all the drives to accomplish, to excel and to procreate.

Throughout his life, the male will have continued maintenance of his muscles and bone, and a number of other organ systems because of testosterone production. Opposite to the positive estrogen effect in the female on lipid metabolism, the cholesterol in the bloodstream could be adversely affected. There are many other things of course that influence this as well. Hereditary tendencies, lack of exercise, poor dietary planning and intake and smoking are some of the factors. However, his testosterone production is a part of these adverse changes. The LDL fraction, if it increases, and if the HDL levels fall, could lead to progressive arteriosclerotic change in arteries. The arteries in the heart known as the coronary vessels are affected particularly, and cardiac disease will result. If the individual is either obese, diabetic, hypertensive, smokes or has a strong family history of arteriosclerotic vessel and heart disease, or has any combination of these factors, that individual could well succumb to illness and then death from cardiac accident or stroke, providing no other accidental or disease condition takes place beforehand. Testosterone has no sparing effect.

It has been stated in the medical literature that just being a male is a contributing factor to coronary heart disease. This is a very sobering thought. It brings to mind however, that this is so very characteristic of many other forms of life in the world. The female generally outlives the male and has the opportunity to better her prolonged life if she takes certain steps. For all that she suffers with menstrual dysfunction, childbearing, and gynecologic illness, the female because of estrogen production really has the advantage.

CHAPTER 3 OVERVIEW

- *Testosterone is produced at puberty in the young male*

- *Testosterone influences body development and other functions such as fertility, sexual drive and performance, red blood cell production and lipid profile, and muscle strength.*

- *Testosterone has many important functions during a man's lifetime but it can contribute to his death from cardiovascular disease*

Your Doctor's Evaluation of You For a Feminization Program

Let's talk about the initial approaches your physician will utilize in preparing you for the use of hormones.

Very probably, you are in excellent health with no significant medical history and are able to use a hormonal regimen with no intrusion or alteration in your health status. But you and your physician must be certain. Your doctor will want to make inquiry about your past medical and surgical history and will make inquiry as well into various aspects of health, of disease occurrence and mode of death of various family members. **_This is very important_**. Certain disorders that tend to occur in families must be discussed. I refer to diseases such as hypertension, heart disease, particularly arteriosclerotic disease, diabetes, obesity, and liver disorders. Your doctor will also make inquiry into your alcohol, drug and tobacco use. You should be prepared before going into the doctor's office for that kind of inquiry, hence make appropriate investigation into your family history. You should know completely and be able to relate fully and accurately your own past medical and surgical experiences.

Your physical exam should be a very complete one. Your doctor should do a complete evaluation of your eye grounds for the retinal area (or the back of the eye) for it can tell a great deal about certain types of diseases, or the potential for developing them. He or she should also conduct a careful neurologic exam and inspect the lower extremities for vein incompetency. Your doctor should examine the thyroid area to be sure that there are no enlargements. Close attention to blood pressure and weight are very important. Blood pressure measurements in each arm and weight determination are essentials not only in the initial evaluation but in every examination thereafter. Evaluation of your heart and lungs is necessary and your abdomen must be evaluated to be sure that there are no enlargements, or any change in liver size.

The doctor should take time to evaluate the genitalia. Testicular size is important to evaluate in the initial examination and to compare later on with a special technique that urologists routinely use. There are wooden or plastic ovoids that can be used for this comparison. Measurements of your breasts, hips, waist and buttocks areas are also important to record as baseline in order to evaluate physical change in these areas once hormones are started. A rectal exam should be done to evaluate prostate size and smoothness (or lack of nodularity.) A PSP blood test should be included in the blood studies that will be ordered.

Blood evaluations must be done to insure good health and to detect any alteration once the hormonal regimen is started. General studies include the basic profile done to rule out blood cell abnormalities, and evaluation of kidney function and liver activity are necessary. It will be necessary that your doctor conduct a lipid profile which includes cholesterol, triglycerides, and HDL and LDL determinations. Evaluation of the thyroid is done with certain blood tests, and serum electrolytes as well as serum calcium, phosphorus and blood sugar are equally important. A complete urinalysis should be done as well.

Special studies wherein your doctor measures follicle stimulating hormone and luteinizing hormone in the bloodstream, and blood estrogen evaluation can be done, but these need not be repeated studies. They are expensive and aren't necessary in the follow up testing. More important will be the baseline serum testosterone. Subsequent tests of serum testosterone help evaluate the suppressive effect of the estrogen regimen.

A very important baseline study is the serum prolactin level. Genetic males make prolactin, a pituitary hormone, as do genetic females, but not in comparable amounts. Virtually every genetic male, however, when taking estrogen will have elevation of the serum prolactin, and that is acceptable up to a point. When those levels become too high (and your doctor's testing will help to determine this), you will need evaluation as to whether or not this indicates just the simple effect of estrogen upon pituitary function, or whether it may be referable to changes in the pituitary known as hyperplasia or possibly the development of a pituitary tumor. Thankfully this is a very rare condition, but a special protocol for evaluating just what is to be done with prolactin elevations is available to your physician in the medical literature.

Studies as are indicated relative to the general health concerns are of course part of this initial baseline evaluative approach. Some of these studies may be necessary to repeat in the monitoring to come, once on hormones. Special testing relative to heart, liver, vein competency, various scan techniques, EKG's, cardiac stress testing and the like, all must be a part of the initial or ongoing assessment of your general health as your doctor feels it important. Your doctor's responsibility involves not only just prescribing contragender hormonal therapy but also maintaining your overall health and being aware whenever changes that are adverse, take place. In many instances, the doctor managing this hormone regimen is not the doctor responsible for the Trans person's overall health status. There are many reasons for this. The ideal is that these doctors are one and the same physician. When this ideal is not realized, the two professionals you engage should share information in order to insure your proper evaluation and continued care. While most transgendered individuals can use contragender hormones quite safely, a few will have changes in their health status that is adverse and for some, these may be very serious. They must be identified and managed appropriately. This means that you have just as much responsibility to keep your periodic monitoring appointments with your physician as he or she has in scheduling and conducting them *appropriately.*

- *It is essential to have an initial history taken, and a thorough physical exam with complete laboratory studies before a feminizing hormonal regimen is started*

- *The initial physical exam provides a valuable baseline for the periodic examinations (monitoring) necessary while the feminizing regimen is in progress*

- *To omit any of the examinations or omit essential information risks one's health and may hinder the effectiveness of the feminizing process*

The Feminization Process

"Tissue response and time are just as important to consider as is the hormone and the dose—perhaps more."

One fact that is important to emphasize when treating the genetic male with feminizing hormones is that you and your physician are really tampering with systems that have been in place for all of your life to this point. More important, testosterone, a mighty influence has been in place since the start of your puberty. The changes in muscular build, hand and foot size, torso shape, voice pitch, and hair distribution, to mention a few, are very well established. Testosterone is a very potent hormone. To reverse all its effects entirely will not be possible for most of you. In addition, your genetic inheritance is biologically male.

In a similar way, the genetic female has factors in motion to account for her physical appearance, that are genetic as well as hormonal. She is lighter, smaller, and shorter. Her facial features are finer and her skeletal development is quite different from genetic males in some ways. At puberty she has had activity of growth hormone, prolactin, cortisone from the adrenal gland, thyroid hormone and even insulin, as well as her own estrogen, to promote breast growth. Think of it! The genetic male has only estrogen and an anti-androgen to take to feminize his body, and this most often later in life and in the face of the testosterone produced by him for long years before introducing an estrogen regimen. In addition, tissue response for the male may not be at all as efficient as in the genetic female. Remember the concept of receptors on cell surfaces that was mentioned earlier - males may not have as many hormone specific receptors in certain tissues as do genetic females - for instance in the breast. In addition, the genetic heritage is not there for certain changes, i.e. skeletal configuration and development. So a sense of reality must be kept in mind by both you and your physician. Response may not always be as one hopes for, expects or fantasizes about, and prediction is not possible. Only time will tell the extent and efficiency of feminization.

With a sense of reasonable expectation, these are the results to be expected on a feminizing hormonal regimen:

Breast Development

A notable increase in the size in your breasts could be expected in the first year on an adequate hormonal regimen. The measurements of the breasts should be measured at each doctor's visit and recorded. *(A guide to measurement taking can be found on page 89).*

In the next year, an appreciable increase could be expected as well with appropriate change in the areola appearance and size. The nipple, however, does not change very much. In general, growth for most may be just a little less than in the genetic female. Sensitivity and tenderness will be intermittent and variable. All patients should wait for about two years of therapy to pass before considering any surgical breast augmentation procedures. Once again, it is tissue response that is important, and not all individuals will have comparable growth even when using the same hormones and dosage.

Early in treatment, just behind the nipple, there will be changes that mimic a small tumor. Don't be worried about this. This relatively temporary change has to do with an increase in the size of the ductal system behind the nipple. It becomes less noticeable in time. The pigmented circular tissue in which the nipple is centered is called the **areola**. This can be expected to increase in size and to become somewhat darker. Some glands in its outer margin called **Montgomery Glands** will be more apparent with stimulation.

Skin

The skin becomes smoother and softer, and if the patient has had electrolysis for facial hair, the skin there will be quite velvety. This will be apparent all over the body in time, on the trunk and the extremities as well on the face. Previous scarring from acne infections in the teens and the aftermath of too vigorous an electrolysis program will detract somewhat from this softening but medical and surgical techniques can help this with use of peels and dermabrasion. The loss of facial hair through electrolysis is an advantage to the appearance of the skin that is under estrogen influence.

Fat Distribution

Gradually there will be a change in subcutaneous fat distribution. More deposition will be evident on the hips and on the derriere. This is a long term and gradual effect which can take three or four years to see optimal results. The waist does not change, hence the narrow waistline of the female is not going to result. Measurements of the waist, hips, and fanny area should be made during your periodic doctor visits. To demonstrate this slow but distinct alteration, continued measurements of the hip and waist should in time show the change in hip/waist ratio.

Genitalia

Generally, there is some shortening of the **penis**, and while occasional authors in the medical literature state that this does not happen, it is definitely evident in many individuals. It does have importance. If the male-to-female individual chooses to have genital reassignment surgery, this potential penile shrinkage may determine the selection of the appropriate technique for creation of the new vagina. Penile length is important tissue to line the new vagina, and it will have some importance in how the surgeon plans to construct that new organ. Skin grafts may be of necessity and that is a discussion one must have with their surgeon.

The individual's **testes** will diminish in size and in volume. Histologic studies in the literature report definite changes are evident in certain cellular constituents. For instance, those cells that are responsible for production of testosterone and those that have to do with the development of sperm are severely affected and altered by estrogen use. All of this is evident in the ejaculate, the fluid that comes from the penis with sexual relations or masturbation. The volume of the ejaculate is notably reduced and may even at times be negligible or absent. This happens because of estrogen's effect upon the prostate, seminal vesicles and other structures that are responsible for the production of this fluid. Sperm counts will be lowered as well.

The *testes* can be measured. Urologists have a technique using wooden or plastic ovoids to make comparison with the patient's testes, and the size of your testes and penis should be measured as well with periodic visits and recorded.

Prostate Gland

As mentioned before, the **prostate gland** is reduced in size, and older M-F individuals who have some urinary complaints because of benign prostatic enlargement prior to the use of estrogen, will report improvement in urinary function once estrogen is begun. When they take estrogenic medication, the start of urination is easier, and the caliber of the urinary stream is increased. Dribbling due to sphincter incompetency may not totally disappear but can improve notably. Urinary habits, particularly those experienced at night can be modified for the better in many. Your doctor should be conducting rectal examinations as well as obtaining a special blood test called a PSA, once a year or more often if indicated. While there is a suspicion that estrogen can be protective to the prostate from the standpoint of cancer development, we still need a controlled long-term study that hopefully will be done one day showing the prophylactic value of estrogen against not only malignant but benign prostate disease. Some data has been published by the Amsterdam Free University Hospital to support the protection afforded this organ.

Lipid Profile

Serum cholesterol, triglycerides, the lipoprotein substances LDL and HDL which transport cholesterol, are all part of the **lipid profile**. By and large, testing of this sort could indicate that the M-F person benefits as does the genetic female taking estrogen. All other influences on cholesterol, namely genetic and familial influence, diet, exercise, and smoking habits, are still important factors to be considered. The last three are very controllable and attention must be given to them for the successful management of your overall health. Estrogen cannot be expected to do it all for the M-F person, but it can be of great help in reducing arteriosclerotic plaque disease and cardiovascular attacks.

Bone Mass

For genetic males using estrogen, a benefit that is subtle, and it would appear, long term, is a preservation of bone mass. Studies are preliminary but strongly indicate that estrogen mediates this in the absence of testosterone. Hence, osteoporosis and all the harm to the skeletal systems it imposes, will be retarded or absent as long as the hormone is in use.

Prevention of Alzheimer's Disease

To date, there are not studies reported to indicate that estrogen using genetic males have the same potential for avoiding or diminishing the severity of Alzheimer's Disease as noted in genetic females. Until such a study is undertaken, we can only suspect that this is true. If, however, other benefits come to the genetic male as they do to genetic females when both are on estrogens, once could believe strongly that this is the case.

Estrogen will NOT produce the following changes:

Female Figure & Voice

Often the M-F transgender person fantasizes a beautiful female figure and a lovely, lilting feminine voice, both resulting from hormone use. Be assured, neither will happen. The waist does not become narrower but stays the same or may even increase due to weight gain. It is the slow shift of fat deposits to the hips that gives the appearance that the waist is becoming smaller.

✕✕✕

Currently surgery to remove the 11th and 12th ribs on both sides of the trunk is the only way to permanently minimize the waist measurements and create a more feminine torso. (At this time, only my surgical center, TSMC, is performing this procedure using a minimally invasive method pioneered by one of our surgeons.)

Vocal Cords

These voice-producing organs once altered by testosterone production in the pubertal years will not change, hence the deep masculine voice remains.

Vocal training and voice box surgery can be considered to alter voice pitch. A voice therapist can be very helpful and should be consulted. There are many benefits to voice training even if surgery is sought after eventually. Ultimately, voice pitch surgery, while it carries notable success along with failure for some, can be extremely helpful for the M-F individual. Sometimes the two approaches are necessary together.

CHAPTER 5 OVERVIEW

- *Expect good progress when you are on an adequate contragender hormone regimen, but don't look for unrealistic and unobtainable results*

- *In time, changes to skin, breasts, hips and derriere will be evident*

- *Voice pitch and waist size will not be feminized on a hormonal regimen*

- *Many body systems will be influenced by estrogen use much like they are with the genetic female*

Anti-Androgens

A very important class of medications to be considered in the feminization process is those medications that block production or utilization of androgens. Testosterone is the most notable of the androgenic hormones made in the bodies of both genetic males and genetic females. Testosterone is made in the testes and ovaries of each and the adrenal glands of both. Genetic programming determines how much is produced in both the male and female.

Synthetically produced medications have been made that block testosterone at different sites or levels in the body in the genetic male. That blockade can be either at sites where it is made or after it is made at sites where it is incorporated into the cells it is supposed to influence. Some medications work more to block testicular production. Some block adrenal contribution to the testosterone levels in the blood. Other medications affect the testosterone production of both glands while some block conversion to more active androgenic forms. The end result is that an anti-androgen reduces the amount of testosterone circulating in the bloodstream. With lowered testosterone influence estrogen in the blood has more opportunity to feminize. It's quite logical in principal and, in fact, in clinical results, individuals on anti-androgens can accomplish more in their feminization regimen. In fact, in certain instances, some individuals can lower estrogen dosage when health status will be better maintained on lower dosage.

Hormonal regimens in the past, relied upon the weak testosterone suppressant capabilities of estrogen and progesterone. Now, we have an important and more efficient class of medications to do that task. Eliminating testosterone as effectively as these medications do, allows the circulating estrogen to do what is intended—feminize. More information about these medications is found in Chapter 10. There is no doubt that other considerations come into the management process with introduction of such medications. They do have other body system influences. But most use them very comfortably and successfully. Many physicians never consider them. You should and you should prompt discussion about their inclusion in your regimen.

CHAPTER 6 OVERVIEW

- *To feminize more effectively it is most helpful to combine the feminizing regimen with an anti-androgen*

- *An anti-androgen suppresses the testerone level in the blood, allowing feminization to be uninhibited*

- *These indications have their own influence upon health and must be selected and monitored by a physician knowing about them and their potential*

- *Your physician may not fully understand the value of an anti-androgen in the regimen*

Possible Annoyances and Problems on an Estrogen Regimen

Weight Gain

Most individuals will experience some change, generally an increase, in their weight. Counseling and instruction in reference to shopping for food, its preparation, and calorie counting will be very necessary. For some, a dietitian in consultation may be needed. I am not referring to problems of fluid retention. That is a likelihood as well. Overweight, if it exists before hormones are started, implies that eating habits are faulty. This must be looked at seriously since the addition of estrogen to the body will make it worse most probably. This individual will need education and physician watchfulness in subsequent visits. For some, estrogen use and weight reduction or weight maintenance can be a very difficult problem. Remember that exercise can be a great help as well. Diets should be selected with individuality in mind, not all thrive well on the same diet.

Vein Problems

Leg pain and fatigue

This complaint can develop from **vein sensitivity** and from the accentuation of already incompetent veins (varicose veins) under the influence of estrogen and other hormones, e.g., progesterone. This can be dealt with in a variety of ways. Periodic elevation of the lower extremities at certain times of the day and evening, and supportive hosiery are two of those special approaches. Occasionally, individuals may need to use a diuretic to relieve some of the swelling or **edema**. This is a medication that influences the kidney to excrete more urine along with the electrolytes sodium and potassium to relieve some of the fluid and swelling. Low-salt diets can be instituted to control this fluid retention and while they may be hard to follow they can also be very helpful to alleviate this problem. Surgery, laser therapy and injection therapy can be considered to improve the competency of the superficial venous system in the lower extremities. Vascular surgeons can be consulted for this.

Phlebitis

The real problem with hormonal therapy for a certain percentage of users however, is **phlebitis** (vein inflammation). This may or may not be associated with blood clot to the lungs (**embolism**). Age and duration of hormone use seem to be important factors in some studies for the development of this problem, and the statement is made often in some of these studies that **doses higher than recommended of estrogen in particular, tend to increase the risk for phlebitis.** M-F individuals who are under 40 years of age have less risk. M-F individuals using their hormones for over a year also have less risk. For all individuals, this is a very serious complication. Though infrequent it can be a devastating occurrence, particularly when individuals use higher doses than prescribed or are believed appropriate. Guidelines given by managing physicians should be observed. When you use hormones un-supervised by knowledgeable doctors, the risk for this complication escalates. Embolism can be so dangerous that it can cause death. Why threaten one's health and life because of impatience with the process? Safe doses in time do all that improper dosage will accomplish and with much less risk.

In some physicians view, once an individual has developed phlebitis, their use of estrogen is most probably at an end. It is because it is life threatening. It also means the feminization program is greatly hindered. There are, however, studies that do not support this very stringent attitude. When we speak of various hormonal regimens, we will give some attention to the estrogen skin patch and some of the encouraging information that is associated with various products in reference to this particular problem will be discussed.

Your physician can acquaint you with some of the signs and symptoms of **phlebitis**, but here is some information to help in your understanding of this condition.

To begin with, there are two vein systems in our bodies - a superficial and a deep one. They interconnect and they function to bring blood that carries carbon dioxide and metabolic waste to our lungs, kidneys and bowel for disposal. In a number of situations, they can become inflamed and blood clots can develop. Both are serious and it's when the deep system has clots in it that embolism can take place. The clots can break or detach and go through the vein system to the heart to eventually lodge in the lungs. The degree of clot transport to the lungs determines the severity of the embolic episode. When slight or moderate in the smaller lung veins, the symptoms are chest pain and breathing difficulties. When the blood clots to the lungs are many and large or lodge in major veins to the heart or lungs, then the condition can be catastrophic leading to death. Inflammation in the veins of lower extremities or the pelvic veins of the deep system give pain and often fever along with sudden development of foot, ankle and lower leg swelling. There is immobility and difficulty in walking. Abdomen pain can take place before any chest pains begin. The inflammation and/or clotting of the deep system can be subtle and progressive giving time which allows accurate diagnosis. It can, however, be sudden and overwhelming particularly after trauma or surgery.

Inflammation in the superficial systems takes place most of the time in the lower extremities, in one leg or both. Very seldom does it have embolism associated, although clotting can and does take place. The lower limb becomes painful, swollen and reddened. They may observed a streak along the course of a superficial vein in the skin. It hurts to walk. Notably complaints may happen overnight or even over several hours.

The diagnosis of phlebitis in either system requires an immediate and often prolonged interruption of the feminizing medical regimen. Treatment will be based on the system involved and the extent of the process in the estimate of the physician by physical examination and laboratory study. In deep vein inflammation anticoagulants will be prescribed. Other aspects of underlying health status must be taken into consideration as well.

✗✗✗

Hypertension (Elevation of blood pressure)

This can develop in a few patients, or can be accentuated in a few, who already have mild hypertension. In the Free University Hospital of Amsterdam study, the incidence of **hypertension** overall was just under 5% with two thirds of the group newly diagnosed as having the disorder. All of the 14 patients reported were continued on an estrogen regimen along with appropriate anti-hypertensive therapy, and they were managed quite successfully. It would seem that it is a concern to be aware of and to be managed appropriately, but not generally a contraindication to hormonal use, unless the degree of pressure elevation is so severe or other complications such as kidney, heart disease, or stroke potential develop warranting cessation of the feminizing regimen.

Hypothyroidism (Under active thyroid disease)

Medical conditions wherein estrogen is used or produced in excess in genetic women, can often times interfere with thyroid activity, often increasing the size of the gland and its workload. This is evident for instance in the first trimester of pregnancy, and with other states of increased estrogen production. On occasion, this is the case for the M-F transgendered person as well. The doctor must be alert to this uncommon but definite **endocrine alteration**, for it is important to diagnose and to treat. Individuals with thyroid under-activity already in place may need additional thyroid medication once they begin using estrogen, and periodic monitoring of thyroid function is necessary.

Pituitary Changes

You will remember that the pituitary gland produces *prolactin*. Virtually, every M-F individual will have an elevation of serum prolactin level once starting estrogen. An occasional one will be elevated quite notably, and if above a specific level that your doctor will know to watch for, some investigation will be proper and alterations may be necessary in your regimen. If the estrogen is stopped and the prolactin levels decrease to acceptable limits, the estrogen can be reinstituted, although in lower doses, for it is known that the increased prolactin levels may be dose-related. If prolactin levels remain in acceptable limits, then the revised regimen can be continued and only periodic serum prolactin determinations need be done. If, however, the levels go back beyond the acceptable limit on the lower doses, or if without estrogen the levels remain higher than acceptable, then the pituitary gland must be evaluated by scanning techniques. This is very important for it implies growth of the gland or perhaps the development of a tumor, known as a prolactinoma within the pituitary gland. One other point to be made is that the anti-androgen, **Androcur**, to be discussed later, will also elevate prolactin levels. This must be considered when a regimen of estrogen and Androcur are used in combination.

This is not a common complication, but it is reported in the medical literature and when such concerning prolactin eleva-tions do occur, your doctor must be certain that other factors are not involved. Stress, exercise programs, alterations in diet and even an underactive thyroid can elevate the serum prolac-tin. Older age is related as well. Your doctor will be aware of the fact that collection of blood for testing of serum prolactin must be timed, for prolactin production is at its lowest level usually in the later part of the day or in the evening. **Prolactin** production is known to be **pulsatile**, meaning it has peaks and valleys in blood levels through a 24 hour period.

Changes in vision may also take place with changes in the pituitary. Usually the **serum prolactin levels** in the blood are clues to this before that complaint develops. All hormones must be interrupted and special scanning techniques will be done. Medical treatment with special medicines may be neces-sary. If that medical therapy does not produce desired results, surgery is the next approach, but this would not be considered without an appropriate consultation with a neurosurgeon.

There is a condition that can develop that may or may not be a problem with elevation of prolactin levels. The development of breast nipple discharge or **galactorrhea** is welcomed by many as a confirmation of femaleness and, in fact, a significant few look actively to make it happen. Production of "milk" or a substance similar to human breast milk could be associated with the abnormal pituitary gland development mentioned before this. If this is the case, once more, the feminizing regimen must be abandoned and the pituitary must be evaluated. If galactorrhea develops and the pituitary is not a problem nor is the prolactin level, than the nipple drainage can be permitted though periodic evaluation is needed.

For those who want breast "milk" production and seek it vigorously, please understand, this is a very problem filled endeavor. Very heavy doses of medication are needed using both hormonal as well as pituitary and breast simulative drugs. The process is consuming in time, finance and stress upon systems not really appropriate for genetic males. Complications can develop injurious to health and even threatening to life. The process as some transgender conceive it is not a permanent one. Lactation or breast "feeding" is a transient state for genetic women. It should not be considered as anything of permanence for the genetic male wanting to experiment. A great deal of thought should be exchanged between the Trans person and a very knowledgeable physician before considering such a move, and then think it over again.

Sexual Activity

A variety of changes may take place in one's sexual interest and adequacy when taking feminizing hormones. This is confirmed both by anecdotal reporting and research data. We have already mentioned changes in the penile length and in the size of the testes. These changes alone will influence sexual function. With lower testosterone and lowered or loss of sperm development, infertility can take place.

Frequently I am asked how taking hormones affects one's ability for sexual satisfaction and orgasm. Although most who consider hormonal therapy welcome the physical and emotional changes associated with taking feminizing hormones, some are worried about their sexual response and adequacy once they begin the hormonal regimen.

☿☿☿

Changes in sexual responsiveness do occur and continue to increase or decrease the longer one is on hormonal therapy. It is a fact that when testosterone levels are suppressed the ability to initiate and sustain an erection is greatly diminished. In addition, the pre-ejaculate and ejaculate experienced by males not on a hormonal regimen is changed quite dramatically and in many, after time, no ejaculate will occur during orgasm. Putting it bluntly, you can't expect to perform "like a man" if you are taking chemical substances that in essence are producing a "chemical castration."

To some that reality is unwanted. To others it is a "small price" to pay in order to achieve the benefits of feminizing therapy. For some, smooth, velvety skin, breast development, softening of the male facial features and the attitudinal changes in temperament and feelings that occur combine to produce an inner peace that was sought and sorely lacking before the administering of hormones.

But what about the "Big O?" Orgasms? Do they exist after feminizing therapy? For many, they are much more fulfilling and intimate. Gone are the days for many when they felt they were only "performing." The feelings and responsiveness that are reported, although more passive than in the past, are quite satisfying. It has been reported that genetic men think of sex every sixty seconds of their waking hours! Genetic women think about sex a couple of times a day. If that statistic is anywhere near correct than it stands to reason that a feminizing regimen will reduce libido. The desire for frequent sex (once every 60 seconds!) diminishes for certain but the ability to have a beautiful and fulfilling sexual experience is quite possible.

Will it entail penetration? Probably not or not all the time. For those of you who have partners who wish for penetrative sex, that could pose a problem. Penetrative sex will be severely limited, if not altogether impossible. But there's more to making love than penetrative sex. And there's a lot more to intimacy than sex. If your partner is willing to experiment with other methods of lovemaking then only your imaginations will limit each other's pleasures and satisfaction.

Engaging in feminizing hormonal therapy is not to be taken lightly. It is a serious step and one that not only permanently changes your physical appearance but also in time can make some sterile. For those of you who want to adopt an "on again, off-again" approach to hormonal usage, I caution you not to do it. It is not only dangerous but also counter-productive. And for those of you who think you can maintain your male virility and feminize fully through hormonal therapy at the same time, you are fooling yourself and most of all risking your health and your sexual function.

Keep the following in mind:

- Taking estrogen & anti-androgens will lessen your libido

- In time, you may lose your ability for erection

- Orgasm is possible and satisfying but quite different than before

- An "on-again, off-again" approach to hormonal usage is dangerous and counter-productive.

Stone Formation

Gall bladder disease as it occurs more commonly in genetic women much more so during years of estrogen production i.e. fertility years, becomes equally more a reality for the genetic male on estrogen therapy. Some transgendered individuals on hormones feel that their experience with kidney stones has increased on such a regimen as well. There is no reporting in the medical literature to support this later contention however.

Cardiovascular Disease

There is no reason to believe that estrogen has any influence on those forms of heart disease that have to do with the heart valves or with heart rhythm, but there is some concern about coronary vessel disease and the worsening of this process when estrogen is used by genetic males in older age groups. Much of the concern comes from reports in the medical literature of an aggravation of heart disease and increased mortality in men treated with estrogens for prostate cancer. One point must be kept in mind when reading these studies. The male subjects in these studies were in a much older age group with coronary heart disease already in place. Virtually all individuals in these studies were 70 or more years of age.

Information about prior cardiac history of those patients was not given in these studies to any great detail, and in some instances no special prior cardiac study or monitoring was done before the institution of the estrogen regimen. Nor were there any postmortem or autopsy studies accompanying the reporting. The relationship of estrogen use and heart disease in those studies does raise concern but its very difficult to extend information about a study of this sort to a different population, the transgendered. Generally, the transgendered population using hormones will be notably younger and in better cardiac health. They will be selected for hormone use more carefully than the candidates in a prostatic cancer treatment group. They will be evaluated much more closely before hormones are started. They will be monitored more closely and regularly in their cardiac health while they use hormones. Without doubt, older transgendered individuals desiring hormones must be evaluated much more carefully than younger individuals and then monitored with great care as they continue their programs. But reports in the literature of cardiac death in M-F transgendered individuals using estrogen are relatively uncommon. In a study from the Free University Hospital in Amsterdam of over 700 individuals, 9 developed documented myocardial infarctions (a kind of heart attack), with several having died. In these individuals, a strong family history of coronary heart disease was obtained. Smoking was generally in these patients' daily habits as well. Usually other cardiac health risks can be identified. These include hypertension, diabetes, obesity and cholesterol imbalances. Patients properly evaluated and observed will generally be identified as possible risks. Monitoring of cardiac status on a regular basis, once the regimen is started is essential.

Until recently not very much basic research data was reported in reference to the probable cardiovascular protection afforded genetic males using estrogen. Of late, some elementary work has been done to show quite conclusively that estrogen using transgendered males do actually have increased dilation or openness in their arteries, particularly with long term use. The thought is that this is most likely a direct estrogen effect although the point has been made, though not proven, that it may also be due to notably lowered testosterone levels in the blood. (Perhaps both may be the ultimate influence in the resultant lessening of cardiovascular risk in these individual— author's note.)

Another research study, however, makes reference to the development of insulin resistance in genetic males taking estrogen. The effect of this is to allow higher glucose (sugar) levels to exist in the blood stream. This low grade and relatively small loss in insulin effectiveness with no real discernable impairment of glucose utilization is known to be associated with increased cardiovascular risk. There is also a link between these slightly elevated insulin blood levels with development of hypertension, overtime, which can directly lead to heart disease. Should we check insulin levels in the blood stream from time to time? Frankly, I don't know. But perhaps the small number of cardiac accidents and development of hypertension in estrogen using individuals is directly related to this insulin change.

The incidence of this serious complication does not seem to be great, although it is very real. Alertness on the part of your physician is mandatory, when dealing with individuals 40 years and older especially. There is every reason to believe, however, that the same cardio-protective effects of estrogen that benefit the genetic female can be found in the M-F transgendered person on an estrogen regimen.

Liver Function

A study of liver activity in the M-F individual is all important in the initial use of an estrogen program, and it must be looked at periodically thereafter. The liver is such a multi-function organ that measurements of certain enzymes and substances in the blood as well as scanning techniques are very necessary for evaluating liver integrity and health. A small percentage of M-F individuals have transient enzyme elevations in these studies with early use of estrogen, but most revert to normal levels in the blood in a short time. Those with persistent abnormalities usually have a prior history of liver insult either from infection or alcohol/drug abuse, or a combination of these. If these disease states are currently active, or if the liver is chronically damaged by these entities, then estrogen use can be a further insult and its use must be discontinued, if started at all.

The work of some researchers seems to indicate that a damaged liver does not handle estrogen well. And that a healthy liver is generally not troubled by estrogen use and handles it efficiently. Estrogen passes through the liver at different times in its existence in the body and is finally broken down there before it is excreted in changed forms either through the bowel or bladder. Hence, good liver function is important.

Emotional Health

On a spontaneous basis, transgendered individuals will often disclose what they experience emotionally once they are on hormones. In general, most are quite comfortable and, in fact, elated. They are finally on a pathway they have wanted to travel for years. They feel wonderful. But some notice a change in their feelings. They have tendency to depression and negativism. How much is attributable to the hormone regimen and how much to current psychosocial alterations in their lives is often hard to evaluate. Nonetheless, there is a distinct number who report such mental changes after beginning treatment, and the greater number of these lose their uncomfortable feelings in a moderate period of time. This implies that outside stresses and pressures in family, work and peer situations, are often more a cause than the medication. In addition, personality variables in the patient may play a very definite role. The likelihood is that very little of this can be attributed **solely** to the hormonal regimen. Still suicide or attempts to commit suicide are of concern to professionals in their reports to the medical literature. I find it hard to blame medication alone for such emotional instability and self-destructive attempts. I think the transgendered, especially the transsexual, has so much to cope with in life, trying to find congruence, acceptance and stability, that the mental climate for some is extremely troubled.

Miscellaneous Complaints

A number of lesser concerns may be evident as the hormonal regimen continues. Individuals sometimes experience a number of gastrointestinal disorders such as nausea or abdominal pain. Digestive and elimination problems may develop with estrogen, especially when using oral preparations. Skin rash, localized or generalized, nail brittleness and fluid retention, are all occasional complaints. Infrequently, an individual may have problems with glasses requiring periodic examinations or may show inability to wear contact lens because of changes in the front-to-back diameter of the globe of the eye. Headaches take place with hormone use in both genetic females and genetic males. If very difficult and unrelenting, the hormones should be stopped for a time to determine a relationship between this complaint and the medication. Keep in mind, however, headaches can have multiple causes, such as sinus disease, dental and eye disorders, stress and neck vertebrae arthritis to name only a few. Consider other causes always and get a check up if they persist. These annoyances, if estrogen-related, rarely cause such a problem that the estrogen must be discontinued. Institution of a different regimen-a different product, dosage or route of administration-can be helpful.

- *Annoyances, although not life-threatening, often occur with a contragender regimen*

- *Serious problems and complications can occur on a contragender regimen*

- *Periodic evaluation by a competent physician is vital to avoid and possibly correct potential problems or serious concerns while on a feminizing regimen*

- *Be certain that your physician possesses adequate medical knowledge in contragender hormonal care and treatment.*

- *If your physician lacks adequate knowledge in treatment and management—get another physician!*

Hormones and Heart Disease— Research Observations of Rebecca Anne Allison, M.D.

In my cardiology practice, I have observed the same patterns of disease incidence as my colleagues: prior to menopause, females have a much lower incidence of coronary heart disease than males. We may infer that female sex hormones convey a protective effect against cardiovascular disease. This inference is confirmed by large studies such as the Nurses' Health Study (1), designed to follow women with no known coronary disease prospectively. 48,470 postmenopausal nurses were enrolled in this study. The risk for significant coronary artery disease was found to be twice as great in those women who did not take hormone replacement therapy. How do these findings relate to hormonal treatment of male to female transsexuals?

Three Cardiovascular Effects

I will discuss the effects of estrogen and progestins on three aspects of cardiovascular physiology. The effect most recognized as beneficial is the effect on blood lipids - primarily cholesterol and its components. Elevated levels of LDL-cholesterol (low density lipoprotein cholesterol) lead to incorporation of cholesterol into the endothelium (internal lining) of the blood vessels, which begins an atherosclerotic plaque. HDL-cholesterol (high density lipoprotein cholesterol) has an opposite effect, promoting clearance of the harmful LDL cholesterol from the blood and aiding regression of plaque.

The effects of estrogen on blood clotting are more controversial. A study published more than twenty years ago, the Coronary Drug Project (2), evaluated the effects of five different drug regimens which were considered to have beneficial effects on cholesterol levels. Two of those drug regimens involved estrogen, and the study showed an increased tendency to thromboembolic (blood clotting) disorders. I will discuss the reasons this study should not be extrapolated to today's treament of male to female transsexuals. Some effects of estrogen may even promote thrombolysis (dissolving of blood clots).

Finally I will mention estrogen effects on vasoreactivity: the ability of the blood vessels to dilate and constrict appropriately in response to stimuli. The loss of normal vasoreactivity or vasomotor tone is associated with both an increased incidence of hypertension, and an increased tendency to endothelial dysfunction and atherosclerosis.

Does the Data Apply to Transsexuals?

Of course, most published data on the effects of female sex hormones on the cardiovascular system have been from studies performed on genetic females, rather than male to female transsexuals. One could question whether these studies are applicable to the transsexual population. Evidence suggests that they are, certainly in respect to vasoreactivity, and probably in respect to cholesterol.

Lipids (Cholesterol, Triglycerides)

The PEPI (Postmenopausal Estrogen/Progestin Intervention) Trial (3) comprised three treatment arms: estrogen alone; estrogen with medroxyprogesterone acetate (Provera); and estrogen with micronized progesterone. The LDL cholesterol was lowered in all treatment groups. The HDL cholesterol was higher in all groups, but the highest levels were obtained in women taking estrogen alone or with micronized progesterone. Numerous other studies have confirmed the PEPI findings. In the August 28, 1997, New England Journal of Medicine, a study compared estrogen and progesterone with simvastatin, a standard drug treatment to lower cholesterol. It was found that estrogen increased HDL cholesterol comparably to simvastatin, and reduced both LDL-cholesterol and

Lp(a), another lipoprotein which increases cardiac risk. (4) When we consider the unquestionable benefits of lowering LDL-cholesterol, proven in many large scale trials, it becomes clear that estrogen therapy may play a beneficial role in preventing the cardiovascular complications of hypercholesterolemia.

Most studies indicate that estrogen increases plasma triglyceride levels. The significance of an elevated triglyceride in the absence of an elevated cholesterol is probably minimal, and the addition of progesterone seems to prevent much of the increase.

Thromboembolic Disorders

It has been thought that the risk of venous thrombosis and/or pulmonary embolism is increased in persons taking estrogen. In 1975 the Coronary Drug Project (2) evaluated five drug regimens reported to lower cholesterol. These drugs included conjugated estrogens in 2.5 mg and 5 mg dosages, as well as thyroxine, niacin, and clofibrate. The estrogen components of the study were terminated early because of increased incidence of thromboembolism and nonfatal myocardial infarction. It should be noted that the test subjects were elderly males with a known history of coronary disease. No controls were established with regard to other cardiovascular treatment, especially aspirin use and cigarette smoking. These results should not be extrapolated to the younger, healthy transsexual population. The Lancet in 1996 reported a slight increased incidence of venous thromboembolism in women on postmenopausal hormone replacement, but the absolute numbers were very low: one in 5000 had venous thrombosis and one in 20,000 had pulmonary embolism. (5) The incidence of thrombotic complications is significantly increased in women taking the higher doses of estrogen found in oral contraceptives, especially if they also smoke cigarettes. This is a good reason to counsel transsexual patients against taking excessive doses of estrogen. Lower doses are much less dangerous. In low doses, estrogen inhibits platelet aggregation and reduces PAI-1, plasminogen activator inhibitor. (6) This

✖✖✖

promotes thrombolysis and helps to dissolve smaller intravascular thrombi. Certain persons may have an increased risk for spontaneous thromboembolic disorders. The Leiden Factor V mutation occurs in 2 per cent of the population and increases risk of thrombosis 30 fold in women on oral contraceptives. These may be the persons who experience complications on low dose estrogen. Other abnormalities predisposing to blood clotting include deficiencies of Protein C or Protein S. To summarize, "The effects of estrogen on hemostasis and thrombosis are highly dose dependent... in general, the balance is shifted away from thrombosis with low dose estrogen, and towards thrombosis with high dose estrogen." (7)

Vasoreactivity

The layer of smooth muscle which surrounds the arteries constricts and relaxes in response to certain stimuli. The major stimulus is the biochemical pathway called the renin-angiotensin system. Angiotensin, an inactive precursor compound, is enzymatically converted to a strong vasoconstrictor called angiotensin II, which produces elevation of blood pressure and a tendency to endothelial dysfunction. Opposing this effect are the vasodilating compounds thromboxane, bradykinin, and nitric oxide, which stabilize the blood vessel and increase its ability to dilate. Estrogen has definite effects on vasoreactivity in women and in men. It produces increased plasma renin activity, but diversion of renin-angiotensin activity away from angiotensin II and towards other compounds which are not vasoconstrictors. Estrogen increases production and activity of nitric oxide, functioning as an antioxidant.

Two studies in the June 1997 Journal of the American College of Cardiology reported on arterial reactivity in transsexual males taking estrogen (8), (9). They studied male to female transsexuals on long term estrogen, compared with matched male controls (8), (9) and female controls (9). They found significantly enhanced vascular reactivity in the transsexual groups, comparable to genetic females. The significance of this is that vascular reactivity allows for arterial relaxation and prevents spasm.

Conclusion and Recommendations

In conclusion, a regimen of relatively low dose estrogen, with or without micronized progesterone, can be expected to confer long term reduced risk of cardiovascular disease in postmenopausal females and in male to female transsexuals. General evaluation of cardiovascular risk factors should include a measurement of blood pressure and a lipid profile (total cholesterol, LDL- and HDL-cholesterol, triglycerides) before and after initiation of therapy. Persons who smoke cigarettes should be emphatically urged to stop smoking, and should be made aware of the consequences and greatly increased risk of cardiovascular disease if they continue to smoke.

The routine use of low dose (81 mg) aspirin in male to female transsexuals, especially over age 40, should be considered, for persons who have no bleeding disorders or contraindication to taking aspirin. This low dose may help to counteract any possible increased incidence of thrombotic events. Transdermal or injectable estrogen may have a reduced risk for thrombotic problems, since they are less likely than oral estrogen to stimulate the liver to produce proteins involved in the clotting process.

Certain persons may be at increased risk of cardiovascular disease, and should have special evaluation prior to the initiation of estrogen therapy. Persons with a history of hypertension should be followed closely and treated appropriately, preferably with medication which inhibits angiotensin-converting enzyme. Persons with a past history or family history of blood clotting disorders should have laboratory evaluation for conditions such as Factor V Leiden mutation.

Persons with a family history of cardiovascular disease should have more extensive screening, with electrocardiograms and probably treadmill exercise testing. The finding of coronary heart disease should be managed in the usual manner. Such persons should not be automatically rejected for estrogen therapy. If appropriate attention is given to reducing other risks, an informed decision may be made between patient and physician to proceed. Several alternatives may be considered, including the use of a more powerful anticoagulant such as warfarin. Orchiectomy may permit lower doses of estrogen to be administered more safely.

Physicians treating transsexual patients should be encouraged to report results of long term followup with regards to the incidence of cardiovascular disease, so future data can be directly applicable to transsexual medicine rather than inferred from general population studies.

Update 1999: The HERS Study and Subsequent Trials

In the August 1998 Journal of the American Medical Association, the results of the Heart and Estrogen/Progestin Replacement Study (HERS) were published. (10) This was a randomized, placebo-controlled, clinical trial involving 2, 763 postmenopausal women with established coronary disease, averaging age 67. Patients were randomized to either an estrogen-progestin combination or placebo.

Over the average follow-up of 4.1 years, there were 172 coronary heart disease (CHD) "events" (coronary death or nonfatal myocardial infarction) in the hormone treatment (HRT) group, and 176 "events" in the placebo group. Hormone treatment had no effect on the risk of coronary events, despite favorable effects on the lipid profile (11% reduction in LDL-cholesterol, 10% increase in HDL-cholesterol). HRT appeared to increase the risk of CHD events during the first year of therapy and then decrease the risk after two years. In other words, there was a clear trend for benefit if patients tolerated the therapy for at least two years without an event. HERS investigator Roger S. Blumenthal wrote in an editorial for Cardiology Today his hypothesis that the early increase in CHD events is due to a thrombogenic effect in a small percentage of susceptible women. Over time, these negative effects were outweighed by the positive effects on vasomotor tone and improvements in lipid profiles.

One very large-scale trial, and three smaller trials, are continuing to look at the effects of HRT on heart disease. The Women's Health Initiative (WHI) involves 27, 500 women with no prior history of CHD. This study will test both estrogen alone (in women who have had hysterectomy) as well as combined with progestin. The trial is scheduled to run for an average of nine years. The WAVE (Women's Angiographic Vitamin and Estrogen), WELL-HART (Women's Estrogen/Progestin and Lipid Lowering Hormone Atherosclerosis Regression Trial), and ERA (Estrogen Replacement and Atherosclerosis) trials will enroll up to 450 women each, using angiography to determine the progression of atherosclerosis in women with known coronary disease. The results of the HERS trial, while disappointing to cardiologists treating women with CHD, are not necessarily applicable to populations without CHD. Perhaps screening for thrombotic disorders (protein C resistance, factor V Leiden mutation) will identify a group at high risk for HRT and give more assurance in treatment of low risk persons.

Progesterone or no Progesterone?
That is THE Question!

I ask that question with all due respect to Shakespeare who
wrote something remotely similar. But what is the answer?
As one looks to the net and the anecdotal information that is
so common at this time, the tendency is to believe that is is
an important component in a feminizing regimen. Many physicians agree but their use of various progesterone preparations is most often based on the regimen devised by Dr. Harry
Benjamin, years ago, who felt that the female's menstrual
cycle should be the model for transsexuals. He also supported use of estrogen/progesterone combinations as found
in birth control pills and prescribed a medication very popular
at the time called Enovid. At that time, Enovid, was a contraceptive medication containing both estrogen and progesterone in high doses—much higher than current day products
and he often used it with Premarin to achieve feminization.

Progesterone and progestins are not the same, although
sometimes the words are used interchangeably. Progesterone is the natural hormone made in the bodies of both males
and females. Pharmaceutical companies synthetically make
progestins. Today, a number of progestin products are used in
various contraceptives and alone for a variety of conditions
and purposes in the genetic female. With changes in the side
chain atoms of the parent progestin, different progestins are
produced having both estrogenic and androgenic effects to
different degrees. Commercially, the most commonly prescribed progestin is Provera—the generic is called
medroxyprogesterone acetate. In general, progestin products exert a variety of changes in the human body. The greatest number is the same in both male and female physiology.
A progestin has no notable effect on the skin, hair, nails or on
fat deposition and no effect upon voice. Also, as does estro-

gen, it can cause skin rashes, nausea and vomiting, headache, libido change and even at times for some, severe acne.

Weight gain because of increased appetite which prompts increased caloric intake and weight gain because of fluid retention are common complaints. Lower extremity fluid retention causing swelling (edema) is notable. Progestins have an effect upon the veins of the body and in the lower extremities which can cause the potential for phlebitis in some instances. Various progestin products have different effects upon serum cholesterol levels and the different components of the lipid profile. The overall effects are not advantageous as with estrogen use. In fact, progesterone does everything in a manner opposite to estrogen. Progesterone can raise the cholesterol in the blood as well as the LDL fraction. This change in serum lipid profile can promote adverse blood vessel change namely arteriosclerosis and therefore a tendency to the development of heart disease. Emotional effects from progesterone use are a very real entity. Some in our community must abandon use of progesterone because they don't tolerate the very disturbing feelings they have in its use. Another consideration very infrequently alluded to by Transpeople in their discussion of estrogen effect upon the liver is that progesterone also relies upon a healthy liver for metabolism. The liver that has been insulted by infection and substance abuse, alcohol the major one, will react adversely to progesterone as it does to estrogen. The most notable advantage to the Transperson taking a feminizing regimen containing a progestin is found in breast development. Natural progesterone is responsible for breast gland proliferation most notably so in the presence of estrogen. Hence, reports that breast growth is enhanced when a progestin product is used are valid. It does help. The question, however, continues to need an answer. In the genetic female, estrogen and progesterone made in the ovaries interact in cooperative and uncooperative ways. Progesterone even has an anti-estrogen activity. The commercial preparations may have variable negative effects upon estrogen limiting somewhat the action of estrogen in the regimen. And because progesterone can exert the same negative reactions as does estrogen in regard to phlebitis, edema, weight gain, it could be for some much more concern to use the two to feminize. When mood swings are as troublesome and severe as some progestin users report, it makes one pause in the consideration to use the medication. This is not a universal experience but many must stop its use because of depression. For the changes that progesterone brings to the breasts in growth (and I wonder just how much that is for no one really has conducted any sort of study to clarify this) is it really worth employing this medication on a daily basis and in the really high doses employed? So there is the question, once aqain, Progesterone or no Progesterone?

CHAPTER 9 OVERVIEW

- *Progesterone can be used in feminization primarily for breast development although it may not be as effective as other medications.*

- *Use of progesterone can add to the potential for complications i.e. phlebitis or fluid retention*

- *Individuals with cholesterol elevation or altered HDL/Cholesterol ratio may not be candidates for Progesterone use*

Medications Available and Regimens In Current Use

There is no uniformity as yet in the medical literature as to the kind of medications or the dosage to be used for the M-F individual desiring feminization. In theory, the best regimen I believe is an estrogen in moderate dosage in combination with an anti-androgen. To give example - an initial or starting dose of **Premarin** or **Estrace** lower than usual for maintenance would be quite appropriate for 2 or 3 months. It is wise to use the estrogen alone for a time before introducing the anti-androgen. With all acceptable in the physician's and patient's evaluation of its initial use, then the anti-androgen can be introduced, again in lower dosage than maintenance. With appropriate time passage and acceptance of the combination by both the physician and the patient once again both medications can be increased to maintenance levels and periodic monitoring begins. All physical, biochemical and subjective changes have to be in order as the regimen is moved to appropriate dosages.

The guidelines your physician will consider will be your sense of good health and well being, and your gradual, but definite, physical alteration along with stability in your laboratory studies. He or she should evaluate your liver enzymes, your lipid profiles, thyroid studies, prolactin levels, and look for decrease in your serum testosterone to genetic female levels-all as we discussed in a previous chapter.

Is there room for other regimens? Yes, there is, and there are a number of them reported in the medical literature. Some physicians use injectable estrogen to supplement the oral estrogen regimen. Some use oral medication alone. Others will use an injectable long-acting anti-androgen added to the estrogen which lasts approximately a month. Some doctors prefer only an oral anti-androgen added to the estrogen. What is most important is that your physician be knowledge-able and adaptable enough to change regimen and dosages as necessary. When laboratory values, subjective feelings and physical changes or complaints arise that are adverse, the regimen needs to be modified to fit the circumstances. He or she must be prepared to do this and to bring everything back to a level of comfort and acceptance for both the patient and the physician. Some transgendered individuals may have expectations that won't ever be accomplished. Sometimes more can be accomplished in physical change with reason-able alterations in the regimen. Both you and your physician should be in good agreement and in good cooperative attitude to accomplish the best in the safest way.

I do not endorse any specific hormonal regimen, but I do emphasize the need for moderation, for careful monitoring, and for patience. This formula works over time.

Several Points To Keep In Mind:

1. Dosage need not be more than moderate. Excessive doses of a product are to no avail and in fact, invite compli-cations. The medical literature supports this view.

2. Tissue response and time will bring to **you** virtually all that **you** are capable of accomplishing. There is no shortcut to alteration of physical characteristics. Hereditary tendency and tissue response to a hormone is to be kept in mind and time is required to accomplish results.

3. Routes of administration will depend upon physician pref-erence and past experience. There is available a topical approach for the M-F person. Oral preparations work just as well as **intramuscular** (injections) preparations in the M-F overtime. The injection approach may be more expedi-ent for some. Oral medications may take a bit more time, but that can be very much an advantage in avoiding com-plications. Needles are a difficult regimen for anyone to experience and mean an increase in office visits and costs unless you self inject.

4. **17 Beta Estradiol** is a much more potent estrogen than those constituents, for instance, in **Premarin**, and those products containing it may be more preferred by physicians in their programs. This is something to discuss with your physician.

5. Try not to make a comparison between yourself and others in various degrees of progress particularly in breast development. You both may be on the very same regimen, yet you may feel that they are moving along much more efficiently. Don't fall into this trap. Keep in mind that we all react to medication differently. You may not have the same level of tissue reactivity as someone else. This isn't to say that discussion with your physician is not in order for some medication changes may accomplish more for one person than for the another. Keep in mind, however, that not all individuals reach the same level of success in all ways.

Estrogens

Oral Preparations

As mentioned, **17 Beta Estradiol** is the most potent estrogen to be offered. It is the principal agent in some of the following preparations. One thing should be kept in mind, however, while Beta Estradiol is more potent it is ultimately converted to **Estrone**, a lesser estrogen and exerts feminization in that forum as well. **Estradiol** taken by mouth is converted in the liver slowly to **Estrone**, hence, it has that tardiness in its favor. Topical and injected Estradiol move first in the bloodstream to the tissues they influence before entering the liver—another favorable advantage. Nonetheless while this advantage can hasten the feminizing process in this using **estradiol** more so than the estrogen **Estrone**, it is still the individual's capacity to respond that is the ultimate factor. Overtime, it all comes to the same place.

Estrace

This medication contains **17 Beta Estradiol** and comes in 0.5mg, 1.0 mg. and 2.0 mg. tablets. Usually, a 2.0 mg. per day tablet is an adequate dose with which to maintain, though some physicians may treat with up to 4.0 mg daily. Increments will again depend upon physical change, testosterone levels, and absence of side effects or impairments to health.

Estradiol
This medication is available in 05mg, 1.0mg and 2.0mg tablets and is another oral preparation that supplies the most active estrogen available.

Premarin
This is a very familiar estrogen preparation which contains a number of different estrogens along with **17 Alpha Estradiol**. It is obtainable in doses of 0.3 mg. to 2.5 mg. with quite a few doses in between. Initial trials with 1.25 mg. daily would be appropriate, and with satisfaction on your part and that of your physician, there is allowance for increasing that dosage gradually, up to as much as 5.0 mg. per day. Doses above this are in excess, and there is creditable work reported in the medical literature to substantiate this. Again, time and tissue response is the key, not high doses. Higher doses with Premarin as well as these other medications invite complications.

Estratab
Another synthetic estrogen that is very similar to Premarin. It is composed of Estrone and several other esterified estrogens and is supplied in 0.3mg, 0.625mg and 2.5mg tablets. Maximal maintenance dose is 7.5 mg daily.

Menest
A preparation much like Premarin in that it is a mixture of various estrogens with **estrone** the principal and most active agent. Tablet dosage range from 0.3mg to 2.5mg with several intermediate doses. Maximal daily dose can be as much as 7.5mg for maintenance.

Ortho-Est
Is a natural estrogenic substance prepared from **estrone** and to which is added piperazine to insure stability and uniform estrogenic potency. Two tablet doses are available 0.625mg and 1.25mg tablets. Daily maintenance dosage varies and proably should not exceed 5.0 mg each day.

§§§

Ogen

This is essentially the same as **Ortho Est** but made by a different company. It comes in a number of doses and likely no more than the number 5 Ogen would be necessary on a daily basis as a maintenance dose. Once again, initial dose and subsequent maintenance medication would depend on clinical response, serum testosterone suppression, and the absence of any undesired effects.

Injectable Preparations

Injectable medications are available and offered by many physicians. The real value of this approach is this:

- Theoretically, the liver is involved in processing the estrogen only once.

- More continuous and constant estrogenic effect is obtained by this more direct route of administration.

Often physicians use this approach to hasten physical change in order to satisfy the impatience of their transgendered patient. It can help in this regard, but to rush this process in my view is not wise, no matter what the request or apparent need. The more important reason to consider the injectable route is to test the system so to speak. Often on an oral regimen, hormone recipients feel they are "stuck" and are not developing as they could. To use an injectable preparation in standard dosage every 2 weeks for 2 months along with the usual regimen and to make and record measurements of both breasts as outlined in Chapter 16 will help determine potential for more development. With change than the current regimen can be re-evaluated. With no change, the current regimen likely should not be changed and the injectable approach can be abandoned for there is no more capacity for tissue response.

Delestrogen

This product is available in both aqueous and oil preparations available for short-acting or long-acting use. Generally, long-acting is preferred, and a dose of 20-40 mg. every two to four weeks is ideal.

✖✖✖

Estradiol Valerate

A very worthwhile injectable estrogen. 20 mg injected every two weeks is the normal dosage. **Estradiol** in the blood stream is more effective than other estrogens i.e. **estrone** in the short term. It can be relied upon to produce the physical changes the individual is capable of in a shorter period of time. Once again, however, each person's capacity to have physical change particularly in breast volume and shape is different. Don't fall into the trap of believing that a lot is better or that one can "cut the time in half" to make significant change. It can be dangerous.

Topical Preparations

Estrogen creams are available. **Premarin, Ogen,** and **Estrace** creams are examples. Some individuals will use these per rectum to accomplish mild physical change. I don't recommend this approach, nor do I think there is much value in using these products on the skin over various body surfaces. However, some who apply a cream directly to the breasts will experience a mild change in size and sensitivity. Some individuals feel that application of an estrogen cream to the balding areas of the scalp is beneficial. These experiences generally are observed only by a few.

One topical approach which is of great worth is an estrogen patch called **Estraderm.** Genetic women have used this product for several years. Its common use is in replacing estrogen in those who are post-menopausal. The patch comes in two dosages—0.05 and 0.1 and **17 Beta Estradiol** is the estrogen delivered to the body through the skin. There is an on-going study in the European medical literature wherein both pre- and postoperative M-F transsexuals have been using 100 mcg. (0.1) of 17 Beta Estradiol in an estrogen patch with very favorable results in accomplishing feminization and maintaining it. The patch is changed periodically according to directions, rotated to different areas of the torso, and the only drawbacks seem to be the fact that local skin irritation sometimes is quite notable in some, and that this mode of therapy can be considerably more expensive than oral medication. There are other transdermal patch products available as well. All contain **Estradiol**, all have different product names Alora, Climara, FemPatch. There is no medical literature about these currently available to report efficiency for use in Transpeople, but they should be considered.

Keep *in mind the following in the use of the Transdermal Patch System:*

1. An estrogen patch can be considered in the hormonal regimens of all M-F individuals above the age of 40, either pre- or postoperative according to the Amsterdam study. It accomplishes very adequate physical change in combination with an anti-androgen.

2. According to the Amsterdam study, the patch can be used in M-F individuals whose regimen of estrogen use has been interrupted because of the complication of phlebitis and/or embolism (blood clot to the lungs). A series of postphlebitic individuals have been studied and followed with use of the topical **Estraderm** patch, and none have had recurrent vein or blood clot problems. Heretofore, this group would never be permitted estrogen again. With the skin patch, their regimen can be reinstituted. Numerous studies are in print evaluating estrogen use after a phlebitis episode but one which critically evaluations these studies makes the point that the physician's fear to use estrogen after such an incident many not be supportable.

3. In my view, estrogen therapy can be a continuous one. There is likely no need to interrupt, or use the medication on a cyclic basis, as it was at one time offered to the transgendered population by physicians who followed the Harry Benjamin technique.

Progesterone (Progestins)

Oral Preparations

The products that are commonly in use are these:

Provera
Known as **medroxyprogesterone**, it is available in a 2.5 mg.,

5.0 mg and 10 mg. tablet. Usually, 10 mg. is used in the last ten days of each month, and I prefer this approach when it is used, but some physicians will give this on a daily basis along with estrogen, never interrupting the two.

Aygestin

Known as **norethindrone acetate**, this comes in a 5 mg. tablet. Either 5 or 10 mg. could be used in the last ten days of each month. Once again, I prefer only interrupted use of a progestin when it is to be considered in a regimen. Some physicians prefer continuous use.

Other products are available. *Cycrin, Norlutate* and *Norlutin* are oral progestins that your doctor may choose in place of others. They are equally as effective as the other preparations that I have mentioned.

Injectable Preparations

There is one injectable progestin very commonly used, known as **Depoprovera**. This is an aqueous suspension of progesterone and it can be given in 100 or 200 mg. doses once per month.

Transdermal

One or two small pharmaceutical firms produce a topical progestin—a cream called Progest. You may need to search for it.

Anti-Androgens

The first of these medications to consider is a product used widely in the United States called **Spironolactone** or **Aldactone**. It is a potent diuretic and anti-hypertensive. Taken by mouth, it is given in doses of 100-300 mg. a day at peak maintenance, although in the regimen used by physicians at the Vancouver Hospital in British Columbia, Canada, considerably larger daily doses have been used. Its ordinary use to counter mild to moderate hypertension makes it an ideal in selected hypertensive transgendered patients as well, for they can have therapy for blood pressure elevation as well as the feminization program. Electrolytes must be evaluated periodically since this is a special kind of diuretic which saves potassium rather than depletes it in the stores of this electrolyte in our system. Your doctor will understand its use and the monitoring that is necessary when you use it.

The next most frequently used anti-androgen is an injectable product called **Lupron** (acetate of leuprolide). Formerly it was given as a subcutaneous injection on a daily basis. Now as a depository medication, **Lupron** is given once every four weeks by injection utilizing a 3.75 mg. dose. Higher doses are available with longer depository time associated. It works very effectively to suppress testosterone. There are however, two major drawbacks to this medication. The first is expense, and the second is that some individuals experience a moderate amount of musculoskeletal discomfort and have potential for cardiovascular difficulties. Fluid retention, blood pressure changes, and symptoms attributable to decreased blood flow to the heart, are known with this medication. Unfortunately, there is not enough reporting for this medication in the transgendered medical literature, even though a sizable population is using it. Physician monitoring is very necessary with this medication.

There are other products that have value for a feminization regimen and are in use although no notable studies have been reported to the medical community. These are:

Eulexin (flutamide)
This medication is used ordinarily to treat **metastatic prostatic cancer** and has value in reversing testosterone in the Transperson. This is potent medication and physician monitoring is very important. Potential for liver injury is a real concern and testing of liver enzymes to keep track of liver health is essential.

Finasterid (Proscar)
This medicine is used generally to treat urinary complaints due to **benign prostatic hypertrophy** or enlargement. It is available in a 5mg tablet that being the daily dosage. It is a well-tolerated medicine and very effectively reduces blood

testosterone levels. Benign prostate enlargement inflicts very bothersome urinary tract complaints which often resolve completely when such a drug is combined with estrogen. A smaller dosage of Proscar is available to help in hair restoration. It is Propecia.

Nizoral (ketoconazole)
This a broad spectrum anti-fungal agent. This medication works very well to inhibit testosterone production and is used in a 200-400 mg. daily dose. There is a warning however, with this medication. It is injurious to the liver for some individuals and transgendered patients who have a history of liver disease in the past must be monitored very carefully, if they are candidates for it at all. There are some reports also that **Nizoral** is not effective over a long period of time, and that eventually individuals in building tolerance to it, do not accomplish as much testosterone suppression as when first using it.

I want to acquaint you with a medication not as yet available in the United States though obtainable in Canada, Mexico and in Europe. There is a moderate amount of experience and medical reporting that exists with use of this anti-androgen, and its use in the transgendered population as an accompaniment to estrogen is quite well established in Europe.

Androcur (cyproterone acetate)
This was first used in Germany as a drug to curb deviant sexual behavior in non-transgendered males. It can be used because of its notable suppressive activity on testosterone production in the M-F individual. It is generally given in 100 mg. doses daily and used with great success, although there are a few considerations that must be kept in mind.

Firstly, for some, liver toxicity is a concern and it can alter blood sugar levels as well. The latter would be of concern in the diabetic transgendered person. Occasional individuals also note irritability, mood swings, and fatigue, and in spite of the very effective feminizing effects, those complaints could be severe enough to warrant interruption. As mentioned, **Androcur** can also have an effect upon prolactin and could be a notable concern with excessive levels.

✗✗✗

I would endorse Transpeople living in the States usage of this medication and obtaining it in adjacent countries or by mail, if possible, but a stern prohibitive accompanies this endorsement. **DO NOT** use it without a physician guiding your use of it and a physician who has read the medical literature dealing with it's use goes almost without saying!

Once again it is important to emphasize—the combination of an anti-androgen with an estrogen preparation, both in appropriate dosage is a very ideal regimen for the feminization process.

Birth Control Pills

Many will be motivated to use birth control pills usually prescribed for someone else. Occasionally doctors order them as a feminizing regimen. In the past, these contraceptive pills contained large doses of both **estrogen** and **progesterone**. Because of the increased incidence of stroke and serious heart attacks in women using them, investigation conducted by pharmaceutical companies revealed that the dosages of progesterone and the incorporation of certain progestational products in the pills were responsible for the increase in stroke and heart attacks.

Blood lipids were discovered to be notably affected, leading to serious artery changes (arterioclerosis). A definite change in the manufacturing of the birth control pill took place. Dosages were lowered and synthetic progesterone products with decidedly little "testosterone like" changes to the blood lipid components were developed. Currently the pills in use contain principally progesterone and very little estrogen. It's not a proper regimen for feminization and if used without physician monitoring—it's potentially dangerous. Can there be some feminization? Yes, but the process in not ideal and not recommended.

Summary

The guidelines for your physician will always be for your well being and gradual but continuing physical change as demonstrated in your periodic examinations. Breast measurements, hip and waist ratios, and diminution in penile length and testes size are all important to assess periodically. Laboratory evaluations will be very important, and they must include liver and lipid profiles, serum prolactin, and a serum testosterone level. The testosterone test helps greatly in assessing the biochemical status of the male to female individual. An end point in that assessment is to attain the genetic female blood levels of this male hormone.

Once again, I caution you in that you should not use more than prescribed each day no matter what regimen you are placed on. For example, researchers agree that dosages above 5 mg. of **Premarin** each day invite medical complication. All that is possible for you to accomplish, will take place with non-excessive dosage over time. Dosage should be graduated to the maintenance level. As an example, if we were to begin with 1.25 mg. of **Premarin** taken daily, and there was good tolerance for this dosage, in perhaps two months it could be increased to 2.5 mg. Adding an **anti-androgen** at that point to the increased dosage of **estrogen** would be appropriate. After a period of observation, both medications could be increased, keeping in mind that physical well being, changes in physical status and blood testosterone determinations along with other lab data would be guidelines to taking dosage to safe maximum.

Injectable **estrogens** may hasten the process. An added concern in their use is that they may put you in some measure of risk, when they are combined with oral **estrogen**. There could be higher estrogen levels in your system than is appropriate. To try and accomplish too much in too short a period of time invites complication.

Progestational products can be used in combination with estrogen and even with an anti-androgen as several researchers report in the medical literature.

Looking once again at the role of the **anti-androgen** in the hormonal regimen, we are reminded of a very important consideration. These medications work very effectively to lower the

✖✖✖

testosterone pool in the blood, not only that contributed by the testes, but also testosterone coming from the adrenal gland as well. This is very important in the therapy and can allow for lower estrogen doses, which lessen the chance of complication. This is why I champion this regimen. The hope is that in the very near future the Federal Drug Administration will allow use of Androcur in the United States, for it is most effective in the hormonal regimens of M-F individuals elsewhere.

80 One additional thought —Regimens wherein there are days with no medication whatever taken seem to be unnecessary. It was once thought to be a proper approach in the past but not important to do so currently.

CHAPTER 10 OVERVIEW

- *NEVER exceed recommended dosages. To do so greatly risks your health.*

- *Patience and time are important ingredients during the contragender regimen*

- *Individuals respond differently to hormonal treatment. This variance is based on your own biological make up not necessary the contragender regimen*

- *Regimens and dosages can be modified to accomplish the optimal results on the advice of your physician. Safety should not be sacrificed and should always be kept in mind*

- *Discuss the possibility of Anti-androgens with your physician. They are often underprescribed because their real value is often unrecognized.*

Natural Occurring Hormones & A Defense For Low Dose Hormonal Use

It should be apparent and accepted that a distinct percentage of Transpeople will choose to use feminizing hormones to alter only moderately or even less the effects of their own testosterone production. Some individuals for a number of reasons will not now or even in the future, choose to feminize completely. Some will desire only mild physical change and earnestly seek assistance from a physician to accomplish only that. For long years, both mental health and medical caregivers have refused that assistance believing that the rule is all or nothing. A feminizing hormone regimen in years past was given only to those who would move to genital reassignment or at least live in a full time capacity delaying surgery. Partial hormonalization, for whatever purpose expressed by the Transperson, was not a consideration. To a degree, professionals have retreated from that view and do understand the need and the importance of hormonal treatment with different goals in mind. It's not appropriate for me to detail the reasons for this approach in this work. I leave it to the psychologist and psychiatrist to give insight to each client. But I do emphasize the fact that lower dose treatment is important to consider and should be allowed by these professionals. The one equally important rule to accompany this concept is that medical monitoring is very important and should not be avoided. To be sure, there is repeated warning and comment from researchers within the US Department of Agriculture in reference to herbal medications. "Those who self-medicate have a fool for a doctor." It is my opinion that there are two distinct approaches to a low-level contrahormonal program. There are low dose prescribed medication and the use of natural occurring hormone containing herbal products. A great deal of literature is available to the lay reader about herbal medication and there is a very earnest effort now in medicine to look at this area of therapy with interest, acceptance and involvement.

Herbal Estrogen

Estrogenic substances are found in herbs and berries. They are known as phyto-estrogens. They differ from pharmaceutical preparations, natural and synthetic , in that they "nourish and tone" the female system. Making them useful in treating a broad range of female conditions. As such because of their estrogenic effects, they can be used by genetic males to induce feminizing change. They will suppress and compete with testosterone in the genetic male to alter physical characteristics in favor of developing the female form. They are obtainable in health food stores and from various outlets advertising on the Net and in various publications. As such, they give indication that self-medication is appropriate. The medical community up to now has looked the other way, ignored and even condemned this every growing practice of using such products. However, of late, doctors are looking more closely and coming to the realization that there is value to individuals desiring these products but warning, as I do, that monitoring is most necessary especially in older age groups.

The herbs and berries thought to be most helpful are the following:

Black Cohosh Root
Dong Quai

It is thought that if Peony Root is added then the effects are even greater. If soy bean is also added to the diet, there is accumulating evidence that it has very notable estrogen effect as well.

Other herbal substances that exert some phyto-estrogenic effect or can amplify such an effect are Chaste Berry, Dandelion Root and Primrose Oil. Sweet potatoes are also a wonderful source of natural estrogen.

There are available products with combinations of herbals and berries. Many of the additions benefit other body functions inducing relief from anxiety, insomnia, digestive concerns and pain relief due to headache or arthritis.

Let me stress several considerations. When using herb and berry containing products to feminize, there is no way to estimate the degree of efficacy of the products in aiding in the feminization process. What is certain is that the effects are minimal to moderate at best. If one wants only that kind of result, they can be a worthwhile approach. To produce notable changes to the capacity is not the end result of such treatment. To overuse these products believing that if recommended amounts are good therefore "more is better" is a big mistake. Even on recommended dosage, inform your doctor and if testing and periodic monitoring is requested, do it. More evidence is accumulating that combinations of herbals and prescribed medication can produce very serious consequences. Talk with your doctor!

83

A Defense of Low Dose Hormonal Therapy

There are a considerable number of transgendered individuals who need to authenticate and confirm themselves by some means other than crossdressing. They may consider and even undergo various kinds of cosmetic surgery particularly facial changes and body contouring to come close to the gender in which they identify. Many, many more, however, look to the use of hormone therapy to bring them close to their female spirit. In their desire to use hormones, they very often realize that an efficient thoroughly feminizing regimen will not be appropriate or possible for them. Their work, their marital or family status, their social involvements may not allow any major or even moderate change. To use such a feminizing regimen would risk too much. But to take some hormones, even for a short period of time to accomplish some mild feminization is quite compelling, almost an obsession.

In years past, professionals believed that it was "all or nothing!" An individual in taking hormones should have only one end goal and that was to live fully in the opposite gender role. In fact, that was not even enough. Many felt they must have surgery. Some mental health care providers and physicians still adhere to this principle, while there is notable relaxation in the professional view that surgery should not be necessary. Living in a full time contragender role, without surgery, is acceptable. The T person not planning or in any way able to go to that extent, is thought, by some, not to be a candidate for hormone treatment in whatever form or dosage. However, I don't agree

Granted the evaluation and management of such a person desirous of low dose treatment can be problematic often greater than that of a fully committed Transsexual. Yet, there should be accommodation for that person. In this day and age, that individual can self treat with natural occurring hormone products thereby passing completely professional guidance. Wouldn't it be better to prescribe and monitor a candidate for this low-level treatment to insure better health? Without doubt, there are problems in the selection of this individual for this regimen. Problems can occur that revolve around the management, or more important a relationship with someone. To avoid some of these problems, the T person must share their intention and goals with their partner. There isn't room for a secretive approach because trust and stability will suffer greatly. And there will often be resistance by the partner to be sure. But with acceptance and agreement in the partnership, with preservation of security in the workplace and with a good, effective physician monitoring, particularly in older age groups, why can't a low dose regimen be implemented? Is it still necessity to have psychologic counseling in order to begin this pathway? I subscribe to this, particularly when the individual is in a marriage. The concept of taking feminizing hormones even in low doses can be very threatening to that union. Still the problems are not insurmountable. The use of a low dose regimen may not be applicable to all. It may be that only a select few can embark upon it. But endorsing such a program, in keeping this door open, is recognition of the Transgender Spirit. The need to confirm in yet another way, the need for some satisfaction and allowance to that spirit is a strong support to such a soul.

☿☿☿

Periodic Monitoring On
A Feminization Regimen

One of the very important considerations for both you and your physician to keep in mind once a hormone regimen has begun is the need for ongoing monitoring. The fact that regimen may change in product and dosage, or any number of reasons that you may have one or several intolerances to the hormones that you use, that you may not make progress in the body changes that you are capable of - all these and more should impress you with the knowledge that the first year or so of contragendered hormonal treatment demands periodic reassessment and re-evaluation.

Once a hormonal regimen is initiated the changes in the medications are directly related to the periodic physical examination, the changes in the laboratory results done regularly and careful consideration of how you feel with this new hormonal influence. Your physician will want to know what you are experiencing and to what extent and should not be satisfied with only physical change. Your physician should make inquiry into your emotions and what you are experiencing in your social interchange with others in your life—whether it be family, acquaintances or the workplace.

Your physical examination with monitoring will be much shorter an evaluation than the initial one but it must include your weight, blood pressure (both arms), your heart and lungs, abdomen and an inspection of your lower extremities for fluid retention and changes, if any, in the veins. Laboratory studies will include your lipid profile, liver profile, a blood prolactin and testosterone level. If any blood tests in the last examination warrant restudy, this should be included. Special studies may be added relative to past lab reports or complaints you may voice at this time. As subsequent visits take place some testing may be less necessary and the frequency of visits will lessen. To give example; if there have been elevations in enzymes with no known history of liver disease or injury to this organ those transient elevations can be expected to revert to normal in a short while. If not, the liver must be evaluated and hormones may need to be interrupted. With continued comfort in your use of the medications and normal results in all your examinations your regimen can be enhanced. Measurements of breasts, hips, waist and derriere should be made periodically by you or your doctor and compared with previous information. If you are smoking, your progress with cutting down or cutting out should be a part of the discussion. Instructions relative to diet and weight control are very much a part of each visit. As you progress to a year of hormone use, your visits could take place every six months depending on progress or complication. With visits stretched out to even longer than a year, the same evaluations that took place in your very first visit before the institution of hormones will need to be repeated-that is a thorough physical, all appropriate laboratory work, an interval EKG and special studies as indicated. Your doctor and your mental health care professional either a psychologist, social worker or psychiatrist should exchange information about you periodically. That exchange can be helpful in their management of you and will be invaluable to your progress. If for any reason you must leave the care of a professional, your records should be available to the next one who assumes your care. Record keeping is very important and those records are yours to direct to another doctor or mental health care professional.

CHAPTER 12 OVERVIEW

- *Once again, periodic monitoring CANNOT be stressed enough*

- *Acquaint yourself with the recommended monitoring process and inform your physician that you want it to be followed*

- *Arrange for your medical records to be transferred and shared with any medical or health care professional by whom you are cared for. Information exchanged between all your care providers means better care for you*

Measurements —
A Way to Evaluate Progress

To take measurements of the waist, the hips, the derriere and the breasts is very important. To appreciate progress, even a small amount consistently each time the measurements are recorded is very encouraging. Once a month, and probably no more often is what I recommend. Bring the measurements to your physician each visit. They should be placed in his or her records as well. While I believe your doctor should also take them, in most instances, he or she will most likely depend on you. Your measurements should be taken in the same manner, each and every time, to have relevance, so certain landmarks are necessary to become familiar with. It is important as well to use a soft cloth measuring tape as that used by a tailor or a dressmaker. Stand before a mirror, preferably one which gives you complete view of your whole body or certainly from the pubic hair line to the top of your head.

Breast Measurements

Look at your breasts. You want to establish landmarks that make your periodic measurements consistent. Look at the nipple on the left breast. Elevate your gaze to a point on the collar bone directly above the nipple. Place the end of the tape on that point on the collar bone and let the tape drop down over the breast. You are holding the tape with fingers of your left hand. With the right hand gently guide the tape directly over the nipple and tuck the flexible tape into the crevice beneath the breast. (The so-called inframammary crease.) The tape should be against but not compressing the nipple. Fix that point in the crevice on the tape with finger and thumb of the right hand. (Refer to Figure 3, line A-B) Take the tape away from the chest wall and read it in inches. Then record the measurement in a log that you keep for this purpose.

Once again standing before the mirror, look at the armpit (axilla) to the left of your left breast. Place the end of the tape with your right hand just inside the fold of the left arm and left chest wall. This is the Anterior Axillary (Line C-D). Hold it in that place with fingers of the left hand and extend the tape across the left chest and across the left breast nipple to the center of the breast bone. (Refer to Figure 3, line E-D) It should pass over the nipple without compression. Grasp the tape with the thumb and finger of the right hand, remove it from the chest wall, read the measurement in inches and record it.

You now have two measurements of the left breast. As time passes with continued hormone use these measurements should increase depending upon your individual tissue response. You should recognize changes in size and volume in these two measurements. The first measurement is a vertical one - the second is a lateral or horizontal measurement. Now, do the very same on the right side.

Let's examine this measurement technique a bit more. You may ask- how can I be certain my measurement landmarks will be consistently the same? (Refer to Figure 3) One way to insure that is to mark the reference points on the collar bone (point A) and at Anterior Axillary Line (point D) across from the nipple and on the left chest with washable ink. Position the tape measure at these ink marks. The center of the chest could be marked but it is not altogether necessary. Another question you might ask is that in previous publications, I asked for hemi-circumferencial measurements in cms. Why have I changed the method of measurement? Inches are more meaningful to you. I find also of late that doctors don't take these measurements and that the responsibility lies with you. I think that this new technique is easier for you, more helpful and more accurate. You may wonder if it is necessary to measure both breasts. The answer is "yes." The breasts can develop in an asymmetric way, one breast growing more than the other or even with a slightly different shape. Genetic women experience this. It really means little. The important thing is the gradual increase in each over time.

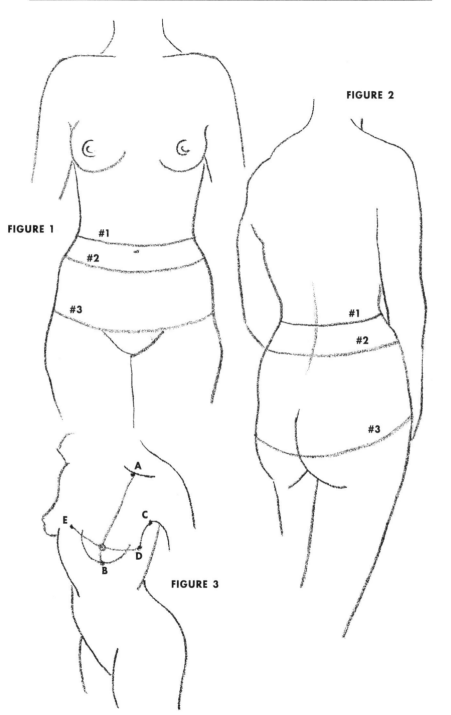

FIGURE 2

89

FIGURE 1

#1
#2
#3

#1
#2
#3

A
E   C
B   D

FIGURE 3

Lastly, after about two years on an adequate feminizing regimen the breast will be at maximal growth or very near to it. At this time, measurements can be stopped.

Waist Measurement

To measure the waist is easy to do unless weight gain is an appreciable problem. This measurement with no weight increase or loss of abdominal muscle tone should consistently stay the same. Place the tape around the body in the space just below the ribs. (Refer to line #1 in figures 1 & 2) Don't inhale. Take the measurement in inches and record it. (Watch your calories, continue to exercise and don't gain weight to keep this measurement stable.)

Hip Measurement

To measure the hips, search for a bony prominence on either side just below your waistline measurement. These two areas are the very top of the bones that form the pelvis. It is a convenient and non-moving landmark. Place the tape measure directly over these bony prominences on both sides as you extend the tape around your body. (Refer to line #2 in figures 1 & 2) Read the tape and record in inches.

Derriere Measurement

To measure the derriere, place the tape around the buttocks at what you will estimate is the midpoint of the "cheeks." Bring one end of the tape to a point at the top of the pubic hairline and extend the other "leg" of the tape across it. (Refer to line #3 in figures 1 & 2) Take a measurement where they meet and record it. Overtime it will gradually change indicating increased fat deposition in this area.

- *Measure yourself in the same manner each time and no more than once a month.*

- *Measurement calculations will most probably be your task. Share them with your physician for inclusion in your records*

- *For accurate measurements, use the diagrams and methods included in this chapter*   91

Orchiectomy —
Why and When it is Appropriate

"If the hormone regimen is an efficient one driving the blood testosterone into the female range then why consider removal of the testes? Effectively, with such a low testosterone the individual has experienced a medical castration." This is a common question. It is a clinical observation that even when taking an entirely suppressive regimen and with laboratory determinations to support that suppression, when the testes are removed a distinct addition to the feminization process is evident. Individuals seem to have an impetus in their transition to female development. For some it is subtle-for some its quite striking. If one tries to explain it on the basis of lab studies, it is not possible. But there is a distinct and observable difference in the appearance of one who has had surgical castration along with a medical one.

There is good reason to consider this surgery in those who are in advanced age or with health concerns that prohibit complete genital reassignment. Without the testes about 80% of testosterone production in the genetic male not on hormones is eliminated. Hormone effect is then relatively unobstructed when hormones are in use. The process is more efficient and the dosages of estrogen in specific can be lowered considerably, thereby, reducing potential for complication. Orchiectomy for this group of individuals has considerable merit.

Orchiectomy in other age groups is more debatable. In any age group if the individual is not married or more to the point not in a sexual relationship or not desirous of one that includes their need for penile erection, castration for better feminization could be considered. If genital reassignment is not a consideration for the years ahead that could be even more argument in favor of the surgery. But if genital reassignment is in the plans for the future no matter how long a time is to elapse before that surgery takes place many surgeons reject the idea of this operation. In the experience of many, penile and scrotal skin shrinkage on hormones can be extensive and progressive enough without the influence of castration particularly when there are considerable years before GRS is planned. To experience loss of penile/scrotal skin when time comes for this surgery is to need, absolutely, skin grafts from distant sites on the body. Hence, surgeons wanting to keep surgery less complicated will be hesitant with individuals with little tissue and will most probably incorporate skin grafts into the procedure.

Frequently individuals ask for orchiectomy even when planning genital reassignment within two or three years. They seek the added feminization factor but one wonders about the necessity for such a plan. With castration in the reassignment surgery the same end will be accomplished in time. And the expense of the castration just doesn't seem necessary.

Is there room for discussion? Assuredly! But while very valuable for some, orchiectomy may not be that all important for others.

Questions Commonly Asked

As a diabetic have I concern about its control with my estrogen use?

There is considerable evidence that estrogen in the diabetic genetic male can make blood sugar levels higher and resistant to the usual insulin dosage each day. Your doctor must know your hormone use and must follow very closely its impact on your diabetes status.

Do I have a worry in regard to developing breast cancer with my use of estrogen?
The medical literature contains less than a dozen reported cases of breast cancer in male individuals using a feminizing regimen over the past twenty or more years. This is very encouraging. It would appear that the incidence of this malignancy is no greater than noted in the male population not using estrogen and that probably the risk of breast cancer is quite low. Does it mean that with the high doses that M-F Transgendered use over long periods of time that there is still little to worry about? That remains to be seen. Does it mean that family history for breast cancer in M-F individuals using estrogen can be ignored? That also is a question that needs to be answered. A study to look at these and other possibilities has to be done. In the meantime, self breast examination and periodic mammography are very important things to do until more is known about this concern.

Should my chromosomes be counted to determine why I am transgendered?
The number of transgendered males with abnormal chromosome counts are small. Most transgendered individuals will have normal counts. The question to answer is should all transgendered persons have a chromosome profile done as a routine. It is expensive and the numbers of abnormalities

found will be so small one should consider this testing only
if suspicion exists in the mind of the doctor or patient.

**Can I take hormones even if I do not intend to have genital
reassignment surgery?**
Yes. There is reason to prescribe hormones for male
transgendered who want to feminize with no plan to have genital reassignment surgery. The number of "non-operative" transsexuals and other transgendered on the spectrum who want
hormones even intermittently but will never consider reassignment seems to be increasing. The procedures for placing these
transgendered on a feminizing program are the same. They
should be evaluated by a mental health care professional and
they must be in the care of medical physician who understands
the evaluation process and therapy. They must also know the
possibilities and the consequences of such a major step. If individuals change their minds some changes may be permanent.

**Why must I stop smoking when I use estrogen as a part of my
feminizing process?**
There are hundreds of substances in tobacco. One, in large
quantities, is nicotine. This drug acts to alter arteries and the
heart in their functions. Tobacco use adds to the hardening of
the arteries process as well, because of its effect on the blood
lipids. These changes can be very hazardous. So much has been
reported in the medical and lay literature about the hazards of
smoking. When estrogen can satisfy such a real need in the
transgendered person and may be so protective to the heart,
why smoke to undo it?

**I want to have a baby. Will hormone use help me in achieve
this desire?**
Definitely not. The male using hormones has none of the essential internal genitalia (uterus and ovaries) for conceiving a baby
or bringing it to maturation or even viability. Even in-vitro fertili-
zation techniques as used in genetic women who have fertility
problems require a uterus to receive the implanted pregnancy.
In a male, a fertilized egg would have to be implanted in the abdomen. Even if it would attach and grow, the dangers of bleed-

ing and other serious if not fatal complications within the abdomen would be great. The pregnancy would not find enough nutrition because of limited placental growth. The pregnancy would not progress for very long. The occurrence of abdominal pregnancy even in genetic women is EXTREMELY rare and associated with great risk and a high rate of pregnancy failure.

Can I breast feed a baby once I take hormones?
Once the breast begins the growth process, it is possible to put an infant to breast and for it to suckle. In most instances, however, the male breast will produce no milk spontaneously. Other medications, and in large doses, are needed to produce milk. If milk production begins, you must realize this milk will likely have poor nutritional value in comparison with milk from the genetic female breast. The milk will be scant in volume and will not be constant in production. The male breast could stop producing if the chemical stimuli for milk production is not constant. And those stimuli are not an easy thing to accomplish. The genetic male just doesn't have all the physiology development and nerve pathways that the genetic female possesses to breast feed. There is another consideration to keep in mind - the male who produces milk could have abnormal pituitary growth or tumor that is responsible for the production of milk. Testing is necessary to be certain these conditions don't exist.

Can I expect my sex drive and my sexual performance to be the same once I start taking feminizing hormones?
No! Your interest in sex will change considerably. You will not be interested in sexual relations as much, if at all, once hormone use is at peak. When you do have relations, spontaneous erection will not be possible. Erection is accomplished by self-stimulus or by your partner. Penetration will be difficult if not impossible. Sustaining erection will not be easy and the ejaculate will diminish or disappear. However, even though intercourse may be difficult or impossible, many report that their ability to reach intense excitement and satisfaction with their partners through other methods of sexual stimulation is quite possible. Orgasm is entirely possible.

Will I ever menstruate?

No. It's not possible. You don't have a uterus to respond to your hormone therapy. Even if you elect to have genital reassignment surgery a uterus will not be placed in your body.

Can I obtain an ovary transplant?

In China, a small series of Male to Female Transsexuals were operated on in this way and in preliminary study they did produce estrogen and did have some feminization. Most of them had failure of the transplanted ovary. The few remaining have not been reported on in recent medical literature.

So to answer your question, yes, it is possible to have ovary transplantation. However, I know of no physician except the one in China who has experimented with this procedure and the results of this experimentation is far from optimal.

Why do I have to continue my hormones after genital reassignment surgery?

Without estrogen after your surgery, you will experience osteoporosis (brittle bone disease.) Spontaneous fractures will occur and your health will be notably impaired because the sex hormones are necessary to many other organ systems.

After surgery, your dosage will be lowered. But if discontinued altogether, your quality of life will be greatly impaired and typical menopausal complaints along with osteoporosis will plague you.

Is it necessary to have all the testing suggested? Not all doctors order these tests so why are they important?

Doctors who don't monitor your health in the correct ways with examinations and laboratory studies are playing with your well-being. These tests are important to gather information about your health and to monitor any possible changes that could affect it. If you don't insist on proper evaluations - you also are jeopardizing your health.

How long will it take to have the full effects of hormones take place in my body?

The optimal results on an adequate and properly maintained feminizing regimen should be seen within two years. Although there is no doubt many changes that are subtle take place over additional years. The process should not be accelerated by increasing medications or tampering with dosages. This can be dangerous and even fatal. We know that complications occur with excessive dosage and attempts to hasten the process. It takes time to reverse testosterone effects and to change tissues with estrogenic influences. If expectations are too high or fanciful and there is impatience in the treatment process, one flirts with potentially serious complications.

Can I stop and start hormones at will? And if I do so, after breast development, can I keep my ability to have an erection?

Some people play at this. It's probable that some things can be accomplished or kept in place with this method but maximal feminine change won't be accomplished as effectively as with a constant hormonal plan. You invite complications as well by intermittent or interrupted use - particularly phlebitis. The idea of having the best of both worlds is not a good or effective one.

If I develop fairly good breast development and then stop hormones will the breast changes go away?

No. The development will stay but maintenance of good breast tissue will lessen. The texture, firmness and suppleness will diminish. In many ways they will become such as seen in the genetic woman's menopausal breast.

REMEMBER—NO question asked is foolish or irrelevant

Write to me with yours or for additional information at this address:

Sheila Kirk, M.D., P.O. 38366, Pittsburgh, PA 15238-9998
Telephone: (412) 781-1092, Fax (412) 781-1096,
E-mail: SheilaKirk@aol.com   www.tsmccenter.com

Self-Breast Examinations

The incidence of serious breast disease —malignancy for the genetic male on a hormonal regimen, appears to be no greater than for the genetic male not using a hormonal regimen. But benign breast changes can take place. Thickening, cysts and strange collections or buildup of tissue can develop and it is important to detect them and bring attention of these to your physician for accurate evaluation. Hence, I strongly urge you to learn the technique of self-breast examination described below and to conduct it once, every month, on a specific date or day.

Admittedly, if you have had breast augmentation with saline or prosthesis, the examination is more difficult. Yet in time, your awareness as to what is the usual in your own breasts becomes very accurate. The technique is not difficult. There are no shortcuts and thoroughness is important.

The position in which to examine is as follows — Lying down in supine position (on your back,) you will examine the left breast with the right hand, the right breast with the left hand. If you are full-breasted , it helps a little to place a pillow at your back with its inner margin just up to and parallel to the spine, thereby tipping you somewhat. Hence, the pillow is to the right side of your back and spine to examine the right breast, and the pillow is placed to the left side of your back and spine to examine the left breast. This keeps the breast on the front of the chest wall and tends to flatten it there. The pillow should not be overly thick. This technique allows you to feel deeply into the breast tissue even with a breast implant beneath the breast tissue. When the breast tissue is thick or dependent (as it is when you stand or sit to examine) you can miss significant changes that are deep in the breast tissue.

Now for the examination. Start with the right breast. Pillow in place, you will raise the right arm over your head to put the breast on a stretch, and with the extended fingers of your left hand, you feel deeply into the right breast in a rotary motion covering all quadrants of the breast, moving from the periphery to the center of the breast, the nipple area. You feel the areola and nipple region completely as well. Once you have covered all the breast in this way, then you draw the extended left hand fingers across the breast, covering it once again, in a stroking manner. This gives you two ways to evaluate the breast tissue: a) with deep point pressure and b) with a drawing or pulling of the fingers over the breast to detect any enlargements you may not have felt with the pressure technique. Now, if anything seems different or unusual, you repeat the above maneuvers to clarify or to confirm. It is wise to feel into the armpit as well. Breast tissue will extend into that region and enlarged lymph nodes found there can have significance.

Changing the pillow placement, for the left side, you raise the left arm above your head and with your right hand, examine the left breast the very same way.

I stress that you lie down to examine, for when sitting in front of a mirror or standing in the shower as many women are taught to examine, your breast is compacted and dense. The breast tissue is dependent and firm, not allowing as full an evaluation of it as you can if it is a thinner organ with the chest wall firmly behind it. You can miss a tissue growth when it is small and in early stages, when you do not lie down to examine.

In time, you will become very aware of any changes taking place in your breasts. Any change in the normal architecture becomes evident earlier with repetition and careful observation. Take the time to be thorough and be mindful of the need to always and periodically examine your breasts.

Definitions

Androgenic
Any substance that mimics or is similar in activity to testosterone.

Anovulatory
Literally means without ovulation. i.e. ovulation (egg production from the ovaries)

Anti-androgen
A substance or drug that blocks production or activity of testosterone or a testosterone like substance. Also known as an antagonist or suppressant.

Arteriosclerosis
A thickening of the wall of an artery with cholesterol, fat, blood cells and other constituents. Also known as hardening of the arteries.

Cardiac Sparing or Protective
Any device or medication that eases or facilitates heart activity. In the case of estrogen, this hormone lessens the arteriosclerosis process in the coronary arteries as they supply oxygen and nutrition to the heart muscle.

Cyclic
Recurrent activity in a particular time period i.e. progesterone production from the ovary is in the latter half of the menstrual cycle every month .

Diuretic
A medication taken to help the body lose water that is excessive in the tissues. Water loss facilitated by such a medication takes place in the kidneys.

Electrolyte
A chemical element necessary in our body for various reactions and processes. Sodium and potassium are very important ones.

Embolism
When blood clots that form in blood vessels both veins and arteries break loose they are carried in the blood stream to differ-

ent organs where they will cause damage. Example: Clots from the left side of the heart via an artery to the brain or clots from a major vein in a leg to the right side of the heart and then to the lungs.

Enzyme
A chemical substance made in the body with a specific task or purpose. Some enzymes play definite roles in digestion. Others are vital in cardiac or liver activity.

Gonadotropin
A hormone that is produced in the pituitary gland and is specific in stimulating a particular organ - an endocrine gland - to perform specific functions.

Heart Attack
This is a general term for a serious interference with normal heart function. It has come to mean a change in arterial (coronary) blood flow to the heart muscle through blockage of the blood either partial or complete. It could mean, however, change in cardiac rhythm (an arrhythmia) or problem with a damaged valve or even an attack of congestive heart failure. It is often called a cardiac accident as well.

Hyperplasia
A swelling and increase in the cells that make up any tissue. The cells are larger and more numerous leading to increase size of the organ.

Injection
Placement of a substance, usually a drug, but it could be fluids, into a blood vessel either a vein or artery. It could mean injection into a muscle also. Various terms that are associated are intramuscular (Im), subcutaneous (sub Q—beneath the skin)

Phlebitis
Inflammation in a vein, often associated with clot formation. It can often be considered an infection or inflammation within the vein.

Regimen
A protocol, a plan of therapy, a set of steps for medical treatment.

Serum
The fluid that blood is composed of without the blood cells. Some substances are identified and measured in the laboratory in the serum only. Other substances are measured in the blood, serum and blood cells included. The terms serum and blood are often used interchangeably.

Sexual Adequacy
The quality of sexual performance. This includes sexual appetite or libido, the erection and ejaculate and ability to experience orgasm or to bring orgasm and satisfaction to another.

Testosterone Pool
The total amount of testosterone in the blood stream at any given time from all sources of production both testes and both adrenal glands.

Conclusion

Medical care is costly-too costly at times, I believe. However, I would caution against too much cost cutting or bargain hunting in purchasing medication. Generic medication has some place in your regimen and is acceptable at some times. Keep in mind that generic medication is not as fine tuned in duration of activity and for therapeutic response as are brand name medications. Hence, while generic estrogen and progesterone could be used, they are not quite the medicines that the name brand products are.

Last and most importantly, overall careful evaluation of one's health on a periodic basis and the observed effects of hormonal therapy by a capable, knowledgeable and interested physician, should insure a comfortable life, with good health and safe progress in feminization.

It must be a cooperative effort, however. Each individual is in all reality "meddling" with their own genetic, biochemical and physical makeup. The individual should always follow directions and keep in contact with the physician as requested or required.

I hope the information given to you has been of help and that it can be an aid in making your approach to this therapy a lot less mysterious and a great deal more satisfying.